C000108089

FACTION! ®

FACTICITY

FACTICITY

—

a door to mental health and beyond

—

ragini elizabeth michaels

FACTICITY 𝕳 TRAININGS
seattle, washington

Library of Congress Catalog Card Number: 91-091467
ISBN 0-9628686-0-4

Illustrations: Anugito Ten Voorde
Cover Design: Graphiti Associates
Layout and Design: Kirk VandenBerghe
Diagrams: Maggie Laird
Book Production: Patterson Printing

Published by:

Facticity Trainings, Inc.
Post Office Box 22814
Seattle, Washington 98122, U.S.A.
206-462-4369

in dedication

to my beloved master

Osho

thank you for my heart

the words

the presence

and the

absence

with gratitude

and love

beyond words

Thank you . . .

to all those adventurers who have helped with this process along the way - those participating in the Facticity groups as they were being created - those whose commitment to growth and exploration of a new way of living was inspiring to watch and a gift to work with - and all those students who allowed me to use their training times to explore and discover their response to Facticity -

to Chiara, Suryo, Rick and Nadine, Ruth and Jay, Martha and Michael, Alexandra and Richard, and Tom and Pat, for their amazing dedication to personal expansion, and their willingness to work with me in exploring these new tools for consciousness -

to Premananda, Kamaal, Gopal, Arpito, Prabodhi, Christo, Chandralika, Ramananda and Almira for their creative input in fashioning these models -

to Waduda whose support in honoring the mystery and the magic opened up new dimensions I´d been afraid to accept as mine -

to Dwight and Nadine for their loving and precise editing, support and feedback -

to Kirk whose presence in my life is truly a gift, and whose skills and vision are contributing precision to this field of work -

to Raga whose belief in me has never wavered -

and finally, to my beloved Ambodha, whose quiet support and extreme silliness keep me going.

Contents

Contents

Preface

Facticity is the result of my desire to share what I've come to know about the value of personal experience. What is in this book comes from the experience of working with my own mind through meditation and hypnosis, as well as working with hundreds of others over the past eighteen years.

Although the spaces described here are not yet my permanent address, I visit them more and more frequently. These techniques and processes can foster and nurture the ability to come to the present . . . to literally be right here and now. We do have the ability to be right here, and with Facticity, we can continue exploring and developing that capacity.

Here does exist. Its location is a place outside of the mind. We can learn to come to this place by shifting the way we *relate* to our minds. This book offers an exploration of *how* to do just that.

This process contains no answers - only ways to explore more effectively and directly the existence of our abilities to understand and to accept. Accepting life for what it is and understanding what we can do to live in harmony, both inside and out, will perhaps evoke the transformation in human consciousness so desperately needed.

It has been said that now is the time and we are the people. With time running out, it appears that we *are* the people. Facticity is for those who don't know what else to do but go on and accept the challenge of creating another way.

CAUTION: YOUR PERMISSION IS REQUESTED!

This book contains paragraphs of hypnotic trance language printed in *italics*. If you do not wish your own unconscious mind to engage directly in this process, you can easily skip these parts of the book. If you wish to engage in experiencing Facticity as you read about it, these hypnotic paragraphs speak directly to your unconscious mind requesting its participation in the process.

Chapter 1

Dancing with Opposites —
The Circle of Completion

". . . *To set up what you like against what you dislike is the dis-ease of the mind* . . ."

Sengsten
3rd Zen Patriarch

I remember standing in the park, surrounded by the sights and smells of fall, watching this little stream I had christened "Drunken Brook" bubbling and babbling on by. I was vividly aware of the earth beneath my feet and awe-struck by the recognition that no-one would ever again, in the whole of time, stand on this spot of earth at this exact moment. I knew that as soon as I moved, it would be over, never to be repeated again. I was thirteen and it was quite a magical experience.

Many months later, I remember just sitting, enjoying an awareness of the mystery around Winter's giving birth to Spring. As I watched the garden's roses beginning to bud, I began to wonder how they could be so calm with the presence of so many thorns on their stems. It seemed a strange thought even then. Much later, however, it was clear the moment of recognition that thorns and roses calmly exist together was a bit of my future understandings already beginning to emerge.

Facticity

Many years down the road, I was eating breakfast with a friend, for probably the hundredth time, when he commented how repetitious life could be. That comment caused me to begin noticing many things — how the sun rises and sets each day — how the tide comes in and the tide goes out twice a day — how the seasons continue to shift, every year the same process, summer-fall-winter-spring — how the body requires that we eat and sleep each day. I began to realize that these seemingly unimportant repetitions were demonstrating *patterns of change* that could teach me something important about how to live. What you will read here is what has arisen from exploring these experiences and these patterns.

Facticity is the discovering of certain undeniable and unalterable patterns of life and their usefulness to us in creating more joyful, loving, creative and responsive experiences of living.

The most basic pattern all of us experience is change — that constant flow of life shifting and moving always, never static or still for more than moments in time. Even modern physics indicates the most seemingly solid substance is, in fact, in constant motion at the molecular level.

More outside our awareness is another basic pattern woven *inside* the flow of change. That pattern is being called the Facticity of Opposites. This pattern is the repeated manifestation of life taking shape through one form of expression and the change of that expression into what appears to *the mind* to be the exact opposite — day into night, wet into dry, right into left, hot into cold.

2

The Facticity of Opposites is a pattern so pervasive and so basic to our life experience that most of us overlook it completely as anything relevant to being alive.

Everything on the physical, mental and emotional levels of reality does seem to have a dual nature. We all experience both good and bad, beautiful and ugly, happy and sad, ups and downs. I began to wonder if this presence of Opposites (duality) truly was a facticity of life (an unalterable and undeniable reality). And if so, was there a way to relate more harmoniously to the presence of these Opposites in motion, rather than continuing to set up what I liked against what I disliked and constantly being in battle?

the beauty and the beast

At some *experiential* level, we all know that Opposites exist and we have lots of experiences to support that knowing. Even as you read these words, you can notice their blackness because of the white background. You can verify the flow of Opposites in the experience of your breath coming in and then going out, your belly coming up and going down with each breathing cycle. You may even be aware of the eye's need to keep moving and to blink or close in order to stay open and focused.

All of us have ideas and beliefs about how to live a happy life. For almost everyone of us, these include a basic unconscious belief that we need to get rid of the dark side of our human nature. If we can just get rid of the pain, get rid of the pressure, get rid of the argument, get rid of anything that is basically unpleasant, then . . . we'll find lasting happiness, peace or love. We seem to forget that spring only arises out of the winter, and the beauty of the stars can only be seen because of the night's darkness.

Even though our experience indicates these ideas and beliefs may not be accurate, most of our *behaviors* still reflect the desire to avoid anything unpleasant and to hold on to anything pleasant. No matter what we may say, we still want to stamp out the unpleasantness, put aside the pain, throw the difficulties out of the house and get the discomfort out of life once and for all.

Many of us greatly dedicated to awakening, personal growth and spiritual evolution report conscious insights and understandings aren't necessarily producing effortless change in our behaviors, or creating the absence of our dark side. In fact, the continued presence of the "unwanted" thoughts and feelings can make us feel even worse, resulting in comments like, "I'll never be able to do this — I'm obviously not good enough – I'm not strong enough — I'm not dedicated enough — I'm not aware enough — I'm not worthy."

It seems reasonable to stop, take a minute, and ask, "Are my efforts to wipe out the darkness and the discomfort bringing me freedom from their presence in my life? Is there something wrong with me, or is the assumption that this is the way to happiness somehow inaccurate? Is there some other factor at work of which I'm unaware?"

Could it be our current way of traveling toward that desired place without pain is somehow leading us astray? The ways we've been taught to relate to the dark side of our human nature aren't generally producing the desired results.

No matter how much pleasure and happiness we create, the facticities of change and the movement of life from one position toward its opposite keeps unpleasantness returning, and with it, unhappiness and frustration. The difficulty is not so much the presence of Opposites as the way we relate to these Opposites.

Our existing beliefs put us in a very confining position because we constantly have to deny half of what it means to experience being human.

We have learned to divide ourselves into the good half — "everything about me I've been told is acceptable and right is over here" — and the other half — "everything I shouldn't be is over there". This causes us to go through life with our good side forward and our bad side back, engaged in a constant battle to either keep the bad side back where it belongs, or get rid of it altogether.

good side / bad side

There is nothing innately wrong in this approach, but it does make walking rather difficult — and the possibility of any gracefulness, ease or comfort remains small. What's more, it doesn't seem to work. The facticity of change forces the eventual demise of any particular experience — pleasant or unpleasant. So no matter how hard we try to keep our good side forward, the time will come when the other side will step out from behind and shift to front position.

Self-acceptance is a major key to healing and health. With this awareness, it clearly becomes useful to accept both our good and our bad, our desired and our undesired. Yet, even with this mental recognition, we can still feel distress when parts of us we don't like take center stage.

This distress reveals the continued presence of an unconscious belief or expectation that the dark side of our human nature and all of its manifestations will eventually disappear.

With Facticity, we explore the hypothesis that when the *unconscious* mind agrees it is alright to accept our dark side, and all its manifestations, we will be able to fully relax and move harmoniously with life. For example, we can learn to relate to our anger as if it is like a storm blowing in, arising out of nowhere, or simply the result of certain incompatible patterns interacting, or like the necessary eruption of a volcano seeking to release building pressures of the earth in order to restore its balance. With a new perception, we can accept the anger, take care not to be destroyed by it, and allow it to pass, enjoying its dark beauty while we relax and await the return of the calm.

By understanding this basic pattern of life's flow, we can learn to relax and allow, without resistance, that dance of Opposites resulting in circles of completion again and again. And with this shift comes new levels of perception and new avenues of creative expression.

The traditional Infinity Symbol demonstrates this flow.

infinity

*P*erhaps you haven't noticed yet how the sun simply allows itself to sink and relax into the twilight . . .

how the day allows its brightness to disappear, as it accepts the invitation to rest in the quiet, dark womb of night . . .

allowing night to emerge in its own time, revealing its own light, twinkling in the beauty of the stars . . .

dancing in the moon beams falling . . .

and when the night is spent, the day . . .

sensing the time for a new beginning to begin . . .

slowly wakes to stretch itself across the skies with a vast celebration of color . . .

night allowing itself to dissolve . . .

resting hidden for awhile in the shade and shadows of the day . . .

inviting a circle of completion to complete . . .

as the dance of opposites goes on . . .

beckoning you to join the dance and learn to relax now . . .

discovering life's movement and rhythm . . .

circling to completion again and again . . .

Notes:

Chapter 2

What is Facticity?

Facticity offers the opportunity to recognize the presence of Opposites as natural and creates the time to learn how to relate to this facticity in new ways.

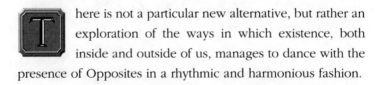 here is not a particular new alternative, but rather an exploration of the ways in which existence, both inside and outside of us, manages to dance with the presence of Opposites in a rhythmic and harmonious fashion.

Nature somehow manages to allow change to occur. The leaves don't go into a tizzy when it's time to change their colors. They don't get upset and yell and scream and demand that they be red and not yellow. They just allow change to happen.

It's the same for Opposites. When it comes times for night to arise, the sun just moves into the womb of the night and gradually disappears, allowing the night its time. It's not a fight and it's not a struggle. We don't see a war going on in the sky with day shining brightly, flashing its brilliance madly, and night creeping up to reach out, attack and destroy the sun. That kind of dynamic isn't occurring. It is a very easy movement from one kind of expression toward its Opposite.

day and night

We can experience it with the tides. The water gets affected by an attraction of the sun and the moon and begins to move in toward the shore. Then, lo and behold, there's a shift in the attraction and the water begins to flow in the opposite direction. It doesn't seem to be a problem for the ocean to allow its waters to come in toward the shore and then go out again. That movement, which is obviously quite natural, is allowed and the ocean doesn't seem to get upset. Nor do the tidelands seem to rage in anger as the waters move away, or fuss in anxiety as the waters comes in.

There are many places in life where we experience the presence of Opposites co-existing in a complementary fashion, not as enemies, but as friends. Many times we assume the lower is against the higher or of lesser value. We forget, for example, the water lily or lotus flower rising above the water needs the presence of its roots, strong and solid in the muddy bottom, to support its journey upward toward the sky. And it is the flower that is actually the root's fulfillment, the blossoming for which it so courageously seeks out the nourishment from below.

Almost all of us have the *unconscious* assumption that the opposite of our good side is our enemy. Nobody wants to be ugly or hateful. Everybody wants to be beautiful and loving. There's even an old saying "God doesn't love ugly". These kinds of beliefs permeate the way we relate to everything.

Deep level change (transformation) has a real possibility of occurring when the *unconscious* mind is allowed to use its own knowings about how life works in this pattern.

Right now, the unconscious mind automatically filters out excess sensory stimuli unnecessary for our well-being. If it didn't, even as you sit here reading, you would simultaneously be aware of all the sensations in your body, all the outside sounds, all the colors and shapes and light and shadows around you, all the smells and fragrances in the air, all the inner thoughts and feelings. You would be so overwhelmed with sensory input, you would be unable to read these words and understand their meaning.

In addition to this very natural filter which allows our conscious mind rest and freedom to attend to what is important to us in the now, there is a second filter. This second filter holds many instructions about how to sort, categorize and respond to the sensory input allowed in. This is a biological filter (it comes with the mind/body, already installed — part of the hardware) giving our unconscious mind basic instructions about how to relate or respond to life and its experiences.

This filter contains a very important directive that colors all of our life experience. This directive is called the Direction Filter and tells us how to relate to the Facticity of Opposites. It directs us to either move toward experience (generally positive), or to move away from experience (generally negative).

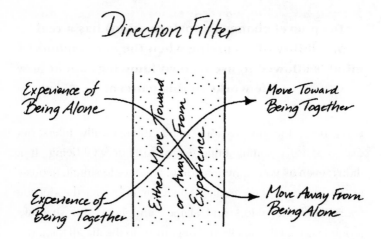

This directive to move toward or away cannot be obliterated or destroyed. It is obviously rooted in and necessary to our biology. In order to physically survive and procreate the species, it is essential we remain drawn towards pleasure and adverse to pain. However, applied to psychological survival, it simply doesn't work to produce the desired results of happiness and mental health.

At the psychological level, this Direction Filter results in behavior that tries to hold on to what is considered to be good, pleasurable and right, and behavior that tries to avoid what is considered to be bad, uncomfortable or wrong. This directive is incredibly important to consider because its power is being reflected in every single thought, word and deed a person experiences.

The Direction Filter is the single most important unconscious directive in determining our ability as human beings to psychologically "live in the now" and "go with the flow".

With this Direction Filter in operation, and the facticities of Change and Opposites being what they are, the lasting acquisition of happiness or well-being *as perceived by the mind* becomes impossible. "What is" always changes and what's more, frequently changes into the very opposite of what it was — love into hate, compassion into anger, friends into enemies, pleasure into pain, life into death.

Generally, there is not an option at the unconscious level of the mind to accept the obvious reality of Opposites as an intrinsic part of the fabric of life, or to allow relaxing into what is the most basic pattern of life experienced by us all the time.

Instead, we are unconsciously working to somehow get rid of or move away from half of our experience of who we think we are, and to stabilize and make permanent the other half.

With Facticity, we are working with the Direction Filter to give us new options about how to relate to the Facticity of Opposites. We will use that filter to shift our perceptions away from an Either/Or point of view toward a perspective that encompasses both ends of the continuum as natural and needed — *both* sad *and* happy, *both* up *and* down, *both* beautiful *and* ugly.

We can reduce our stress when we relax into the present and allow things that can't change to be accepted.

Y our unconscious mind can learn . . .

and cause a change to occur . . .

an expansion of an understanding . . .

a new association of experience that was not there before . . .

and your unconscious mind can sort out all that experience

that is your experience . . .

allowing you to see . . .

and recall the places where the opposites of life work together . . .

like a whole . . .

circle that has a beginning . . .

and where there's a beginning . . .

there must be an end . . .

and in the circle . . .

can you find the beginning . . .

can you find the end . . .

as the circle goes round . . .

and the opposites . . .

create a whole . . .

circle of completion? . . .

Facticity helps us evoke our outer experience of Opposites to help us learn *how* to relate to the inner experience of Opposites in a different manner. Existence shows us again and again how Opposites relax with one another — how they work with one another — how they're essential to one another — how each gives birth to the other. That is the flow again and again. The more we see that and hear that and feel that, the more the unconscious mind is willing to use *that* experience as a guideline to create new behaviors.

The more we become aware of the Facticity of Opposites and their complementary nature, the more we can relax into our human nature without a fight.

As we become more aware of Opposites, we become more aware of the paradoxical nature of being alive. The Direction Filter that sorts our experiences into either for or against makes it seem logically impossible to accept life as both light and dark, both pleasurable and painful.

Facticity

The experience of Opposites *through the mind* does exist and becomes paradoxical when the mind realizes Opposites are actually complementary rather than in opposition. Fortunately, the unconscious mind, through its experience of patterns, can be re-educated to relax into paradox and to relax with the security of knowing constant change and continual movement to be the natural flow of life experience.

There are places where Opposites also happen simultaneously as well as in a flow back and forth. For example, there are muscle fibers that relax and ones that contract in the same muscle. Muscle tone is built on this ability of the fibers in the muscle. Most of them are relaxed, but the tone is due to a slight contraction in a certain number of fibers. Opposites happen simultaneously when a bird is sitting on the limb of a tree. He is holding on while at the same time letting go as the limb moves with his weight or with a breeze arising from the wind. Both are in operation at the same time.

However, whether energy is flowing from one extreme toward its opposite, or manifesting both expressions simultaneously, there is always that place where the energy is changing its shape of expression from one form into another.

Because there is a flow, there is a place where balance can be found. There is a center point at which a person can come to resting, engaging in the experiencing of re-creating balancing while allowing this flow to happen without discomfort or displeasure.

ow, your unconscious mind . . .

can begin to prepare . . .

to lovingly and respectfully join hands . . .

with that vast reservoir of your experience . . .

unnoticed before . . .

important now . . .

to allow a whole new way of relating . . .

to begin being created . . .

and it will be your way of relating . . .

as that center point emerges . . .

more clearly . . .

solidly firm . . .

in harmony with the rhythm of each step . . .

allowing that comfort and pleasure . . .

as the flow happens . . .

and you rest . . .

in that centered place . . .

inviting the balancing to arise . . .

freeing the dance to unfold . . .

and the circle of completion . . .

to complete . . .

again and again . . .

Chapter 3

How Does Facticity Work?

". . . God is day and night, winter and summer, war and peace, satiety and want . . ."
Heraclitus
Greek Mystic

H uman beings are incredibly creative in the ways we experience problems. However, our root difficulty seems to be the way we *relate* to certain unalterable and undeniable facticities of life. As long as we are unable to accept that things we perceive in opposition, i.e., light and dark, love and hate, distance and closeness, are as intimately connected as our in-breath and out-breath, we will continue to perceive much life experience as unacceptable. Life apparently requires both extremes in order to be what it is.

According to Webster, facticity refers to anything that is an undeniable and unalterable fact existing in time and space, i.e., in the realm of mind/body. More importantly, a facticity is something that is verifiable through our own experience. With the Facticity process, we draw on our *discounted experiential knowledge* and begin to use it in a whole new way.

The facticities at the root of discontent with the human experience are the presence of Opposites, the permanence of Change, the unavoidability of experiencing death, pressure and pain, and the paradox of being alone while at the same time being connected.

After years of living, few people will argue the presence of these facticities. However, most of our *behavior* reflects unawareness or unacceptance of what we do know about these experiences of living. How many times do we insist on seeking security, forgetting that change is the only thing we can count on continuing? How often do we find ourselves clinging to the pure pleasure of a beautiful moment, avoiding the inevitable time of letting it go on its way?

This negation of our own experiential knowledge is due to certain presuppositions and assumptions operating at the *unconscious* level. It is the presence of these *unconscious* presuppositions, assumptions and beliefs that frustrate our living in harmony with what we have learned from being alive.

The unconscious mind is the mind in charge of behavior and without its permission, no change will occur.

No matter how much we understand consciously, it is the job of the unconscious mind to protect our integrity and well-being as a total, functioning unit. Whether we want to change a particular behavior, or go for the transformational experience of living in the moment with conscious awareness, the unconscious mind still has to be absolutely convinced that is the appropriate way to go.

However, an unconscious mind must be convinced in an entirely different fashion than a conscious mind, and Facticity is dedicated to this part of the process. Like primitive man, the unconscious level of modern man's sophisticated mind still responds to the art of storytelling. With the listener in an altered state of consciousness and the storyteller consciously and artfully weaving language to satisfy both levels of mind (the simple unconscious and the sophisticated conscious), impactful shifts can occur (see *Lions In Wait*).

Neuro-Linguistic Programming (NLP) and Ericksonian Hypnosis (see Glossary) are among the most modern and advanced technologies and methodologies for working with the subjective mind. With Facticity, we use these tools to re-educate the unconscious mind to:

1. The presence of its own discounted experiential knowledge (particularly relating to Change and Opposites).

2. Its own abilities to relate to that wealth of experience in new ways.

Through the creation of pleasant altered states of consciousness, we can create a space of freedom for the unconscious mind to recognize, reorganize and reassociate its own knowings about how life moves and flows in repeating patterns, and in particular, how it flows in the pattern of Opposites.

A nd as you continue reading these words . . .

relaxing in your own way . . .

your unconscious mind can now . . .

continue that search . . .

discovering just how two things . . .

that seem so opposed . . .

can actually work together . . .

because although that conscious mind . . .

operates on a certain surface . . .

behind every surface there is a depth . . .

and that depth of your unconscious mind . . .

can begin to take these words . . .

that have meaning and significance for you . . .

and continue that re-collection now . . .

of how two things seemingly opposed . . .

really do work together . . .

Facticity utilizes NLP techniques to work with old beliefs and values that are in conflict with an acceptance of Opposites. This work adds to the current NLP model in that awareness of the Facticity of Opposites is brought to every change being made (where appropriate), and a value given to every aspect that was unconsciously denied by the old standard or attitude so that acceptance of that aspect can occur.

A certain amount of wisdom and depth of understanding become available when we begin to recognize what we already know. Realizing a star's light only becomes visible when the sun leaves the sky, could cause us to shift the way we relate to our own experiences of lightness and darkness. By using our existing *discounted* experiential knowledge, the unconscious mind can create new ways to relate to this level of reality (mind/body) as it really is, rather than the way it "should" be.

Becoming free to accept the fundamental facticities always present in life creates a reachable state of mental health and a real probability of creating our lives the way we want them to be.

With an awareness of Opposites or duality, and an attitude of acceptance and relaxation toward them, the suffering can be removed from our experience. It seems there will always be pain and unpleasantness in the human experience, but suffering — that is pain because of the pain — can be eliminated — and the capacity to accept the frailty as well as the strength of being human can more easily be expanded. We don't see a rose flower suffering because of its fragility and vulnerability to the winds and the storms. It just seems to go ahead and open, trusting its strength to respond to these natural elements as best it can, perhaps even looking forward to the dance of its fragrance with the winds.

rose flower

It appears an understanding of how the mind works can naturally lead to an easier understanding of meditation, its value and purpose. Therefore, with Facticity we also include working with the experience of content-free meditation. These are techniques designed to build awareness (witnessing, watching) through the experience of *bare attention* or awareness of sensory experience without judgement or discrimination. (In NLP language, this can be called being up-time to your own down-time.)

The NLP technology of sub-modalities (see Glossary) is a natural bridge for movement out of the mind (mental activities) into the senses. The senses are one step closer to the real experience of life than the mind, which can only think *about* living. When we live in our senses, we are more able to find that balance point from which we can step beyond the mind and the body into the realm commonly languaged as spirit, No-Mind, Samadhi, Satori, Christ Consciousness, Nirvana, the Void.

Although Facticity proposes a new door to mental health through awareness of Opposites at the *unconscious* level of the mind, Facticity has its roots and origins in the study of spiritual seekers and their patterns of response. Whatever else this exploration is uncovering, it is designed to accelerate the development of human consciousness and the presence of non-judgemental (choiceless) awareness.

nd sometimes a person can remember . . .

those childhood plays . . .

in that playground of teeter-totters and see-saws . . .

delighting in the exhilaration of moving up . . .

and wondering at the pain of plopping down too hard on that

ground . . . and how long does it take a child to learn . . .

of that place in the center of that see-saw . . .

going back and forth . . .

recognizing that center point . . .

remains unaffected by the change of that board . . .

going up on one end while the other plops down . . .

and a child can . . .

learn to stand in the middle . . .

of that board and hold their place . . .

by letting go and allowing that body to move with the flow of up . . .

and down . . . easily now . . .

Chapter 4

Discounted Experience —
Selling Yourself Short?

*". . . Men are as forgetful and heedless in their waking moments of
what is going on around them as they are during their sleep . . ."*
Heraclitus
Greek Mystic

 e all have lots of experience to back up our beliefs
and expectations. However, this does not negate the
presence of other experiences that we simply don't
recognize or even realize are ours.

If I believe I'm unlovable because I don't have a lover, I
probably won't even consider those experiences where I am
obviously loved and liked by non-lovers. The experience is
there but not recognized.

When we are born, we begin to receive messages and commu-
nications, both verbal and non-verbal, that start to shape our
perceptions of experience. Just as the unconscious mind filters
out unnecessary sensory stimuli automatically, the unconscious
mind also starts to filter out experiences that we are taught not
to know.

Our capacities to imagine, to dream, to create are already beginning to be dampened at this early stage. We are given ideas and beliefs that become real to us over time. An excellent example of a "learned not-knowing" is the idea that there is only one way to create a garden, and that is usually in rows that are parallel. This type of learning filters out our natural capacities for creative perception, and in particular filters out the recognition of a variety of ways to plant a garden, i.e., in circles, in the shape of diamonds, in figure 8's, in ovals. As time passes, we don't even think to consider other possibilities.

And as you continue allowing these words . . .

to have just the right meaning for you . . .

that unconscious mind can continue now . . .

to let go and relax . . .

knowing a child learns many things . . .

and it might be years before a person remembers . . .

that without the darkness of that blackboard . . .

whether it be black or green . . .

why the white letters would never be seen . . .

they'd disappear and remain unknown . . .

just like the roots of something so beautiful as the water lily . . .

allowing itself to open its petals to the sun . . .

to share its fragrance with the wind . . .

why that flower's roots . . .

deep down in the slimy mud are needed . . .

to allow that beautiful blossom to arise . . .

and lift itself right on up and out of that slimy soil. . .

and be the beautiful blossom it was meant to be . . .

and isn't that a nice recognition to realize . . .

With Facticity, we become aware we simply do not attend to a vast array of experiential knowings we have about life. **We don't usually attend to these knowings because we don't perceive them as relevant or useful information**.

To begin with, everyone has massive amounts of experience that can support an awareness that everything changes. And we all have massive experience supporting the recognition that Opposites do exist and do flow in a pattern back and forth. So, our first step is to recognize, value, and then utilize this discounted information, if, in fact, this is truly our experience.

If I'm not feeling loved and I'm complaining to my mother and she says "I love you", I almost always would say, "yes, but, you're my mother". This is discounting existing experience. If I want confidence in my personal life, and a friend points out how confident I am in my job, I would most always say, "yes, but that's different". This is discounting existing experience as irrelevant.

If Opposites are indeed a facticity of life, then there must be experiential evidence of that as a universal reality. As we gather and begin to value those discounted experiences that recognize not only the presence of Opposites, but how they work

together, harmoniously in a complementary fashion, the unconscious mind begins to notice new information previously
labeled unimportant.

This gathering of discounted experiential information occurs
through the creation of pleasant altered states of consciousness. In these trance-like states, the unconscious mind is more
willing to search for these experiences and more receptive to
utilizing them in a new way.

For example, when you read or hear about the change in the
seasons, it may not impact you in any specific manner. However, in an altered state of consciousness, the unconscious mind
can be invited to make maximum meaning out of what is being
said. In that invitation rests the potential for a new understanding to arise. In this case, perhaps a new awareness could arise
of how the seasons work together to allow the full cycle of life
and death to unfold harmoniously. Or perhaps, depending on
what is being said, a new value seen for the dark, cold months
of winter as the time needed for what has died to be trans-
formed into something new.

As undeniable evidence of Opposites and their complementariness continue being discovered through trance-like experiences, the unconscious mind begins to reorganize and reassociate
its learnings and experiences in a new way. The old beliefs and
values no longer wanted or needed will begin to crumble and
fall away as we simultaneously work with NLP to uproot the
way they are being held or represented in the mind.

If you have a tree in your front yard that no longer gives your yard the look and feel you desire, and you want to get rid of that tree, you don't prune back the branches. You know from experience, pruning only makes the tree send even more juice to its branches, and the next year the tree will actually get bigger. So, if you want to get rid of the tree altogether, the best choice is to take it out by the roots.

Once that is done, you then have a big hole in your front yard — and not only is that probably going to be offensive to your aesthetic sense, it could also be very dangerous. You, a neighbor, or a small child might fall into that hole and get hurt. So, you will probably replant something in that hole and it will probably be the kind of tree or plant you'd really like there.

With Facticity, we can gently uproot the beliefs and values in operation that we have decided are no longer appropriate for us, and replace them with our own discounted experiential

Facticity

knowledge. Richard Bandler, Robert Dilts and others in the
NLP world have created a body of work relating to changing
beliefs. In Facticity, we use this technology to move beyond
beliefs into experiential knowing as a more reasonable and
available avenue to mental health and happier living.

*A*nd your unconscious mind . . .

can learn . . .

from your experience . . .

of the trees and of the wind . . .

your experience of that sky . . .

remaining boundless and expansive behind the clouds . . .

allowing . . .

your experience of just how does nature . . .

allow the cold of winter . . .

so bleak and freezing . . .

to make its change . . .

into that warm, hot summer sun . . .

holding within it the seeds . . .

of yet another winter's discontent . . .

and your unconscious mind can . . .

draw on that wonder of life . . .

and continue now . . .

uncovering what you've been taught not to know . . .

yourself . . .

and that ability to flow . . .

When working with human beings, more change can occur more easily when you work at the highest and/or deepest levels possible.

Because most existing beliefs and values are based on an unawareness and unacceptance of Opposites, massive changes do occur when that undeniable realm of experience is allowed, valued, and invited to participate in the creation of new guidelines for happier and more creative living.

A simple model for the process that carries a perception into action is the following:

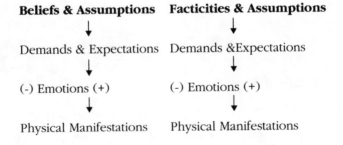

Beliefs & Assumptions	Facticities & Assumptions
↓	↓
Demands & Expectations	Demands &Expectations
↓	↓
(-) Emotions (+)	(-) Emotions (+)
↓	↓
Physical Manifestations	Physical Manifestations

With Facticity, we are working to change only a portion of the model directly — shifting the basis for response from beliefs & assumptions into facticities & assumptions, or our experiential knowledge. Because we are working at this high (or deep) level, its effects will cascade down (or trickle up), allowing other shifts to occur automatically. (See Chapter 18 on Identity and Logical Levels of Change.)

If we want to know *how* to reach a life without suffering, there are many existing experiences we are overlooking that can help us find the "how". Our discounted experiential knowledge is a vast reservoir of hidden resources just awaiting the arrival of our attention.

Notes:

Chapter 5

Facticity Model for Mental Health

". . . The creative act is bliss, the resistance, unending pain . . ."

The Philosophy of Consciousness Without An Object
Franklin Merrell-Wolff

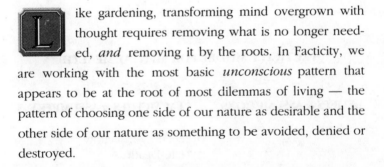ike gardening, transforming mind overgrown with thought requires removing what is no longer needed, *and* removing it by the roots. In Facticity, we are working with the most basic *unconscious* pattern that appears to be at the root of most dilemmas of living — the pattern of choosing one side of our nature as desirable and the other side of our nature as something to be avoided, denied or destroyed.

When the *unconscious* mind understands that it is to the advantage of the individual to perceive *both* sides of our human nature as acceptable and "what is", all the other problems rooted in this basic perception will begin to shift as well. In addition, the mental energies that were engaged in creating and fighting these endless internal battles between what we like and what we dislike, will become free to engage in the highest form of human intelligence I know — the creative response to now.

In the Facticity work already done, participants are reporting changes occurring automatically in behaviors, emotions, beliefs and expectations. This experience of being able to emotionally accept previously unacceptable thoughts and feelings begins to happen automatically, as those "previous problem states" begin to be perceived as natural, part of a process, and simply "what is for right now". This changes the *idea* of self-acceptance into a stronger and more real experience.

Note that the states on the left side of the following model are generally what we consider to be problems, and the things on the right side are generally what we consider to be desired states.

FACTICITY MODEL FOR MENTAL HEALTH

BELIEFS & ASSUMPTIONS   **FACTICITIES & ASSUMPTIONS**

Security-Insecurity
Life-Death
Pleasure-Pain
Alone-Together

The Universe is patterned, ordered and creative and makes use of everything in its process.

Human beings are a part of the Universe and have a relevant role to play that is knowable through experience.

DEMANDS & EXPECTATIONS   **DEMANDS & EXPECTATIONS**

1. approval from others
2. security

3. control

4. goal fulfillment
5. expert's mind
6. to be needed

1. self-respect
2. flexibility (acceptance of change and insecurity)
3. responsiveness (trust in one's own ability to respond)
4. process awareness
5. beginner's mind
6. to share

EMOTIONS   **EMOTIONS**

Highly judged as indications of success or failure.

Recognized as facticity of the moment and explored for possible gift of learning and/or understanding.

PHYSICAL MANIFESTATIONS   **PHYSICAL MANIFESTATIONS**

as
  Sex
  Relationships

as
  Sensuousness
  Relating

through
  Reaction
  Dis-Ease

through
  Response
  Balance

The existence of religions, philosophies, rites and rituals reflect the human need to know that we belong to something, or to know that we are indeed a part of something larger than ourselves. Most often, we are given answers to these innate questionings long before we have even tasted our personal thirst for knowing. As children, we are automatically fed beliefs and demands and expectations. These are designed to give us the *feeling* that we understand why we are here and what this experience of being alive is all about.

Facticity

The traditional mid-life crisis often reflects the doubt hidden behind the believing. Still unanswered questions make their way to the surface. Am I alone on this planet floating in space? Am I all on my own? Does life have any purpose or meaning?

Facticity does not have an answer to these questions. It simply offers another way to explore coming to a *knowing* instead of a believing. With Facticity, we are assuming that if it is true we are a part of existence with a meaningful role to play, then that truth must be knowable. And that truth will have to come through experiential knowledge. Intellectual knowledge is, by its nature, always a *description* of experience and not the actual experience itself. If we really want to know the taste of pistachio ice cream, we have to eat it. All the descriptive talk in the world won't create the actual experience of the taste.

At the unconscious level, experiential knowledge is the only knowledge that can completely eradicate doubt.

ust as you can continue to open . . .

that wealth of knowing that is yours . . .

comfortably unlearning now . . .

freeing yourself . . .

to explore new ways with ease . . .

and an easy letting go . . .

into that unlearning . . .

allowing your experience to fly free . . .

to feed you a taste . . .

of a new height . . .

a new perspective . . .

as radically different . . .

as the sky must seem to that butterfly . . .

so long encased in the tiny caterpillar brain . . .

forced to stay grounded . . .

and your unconscious mind . . .

can continue now . . .

receiving the wisdom of existence itself . . .

handing you that wealth . . .

of your experience . . .

to draw upon now . . .

in your own way . . .

you can keep your finger . . .

right on the flow of things . . .

and go ahead and be in touch . . .

with how life . . .

expresses itself naturally . . .

now . . .

Through Facticity, we can re-educate the unconscious mind to recognize it already knows a great deal about life's patterns through its own discounted experience. The unconscious mind can become free to use the knowledge it already has at its deepest levels. This knowledge can guide the creation of appropriate steps and risks and creative actions that we as individuals need to claim that "ultimate knowing" for ourselves.

**There is no right way to get to these knowings.
There is only each person's individual way.**

From these basic assumptions, we use Facticity to weave hypotheses that we can explore for ourselves. Are there really undeniable and unalterable facticities of life? Are there new ways to relate to these facticities? Can we build new guidelines based on our experience of patterns that repeat themselves in an ordered and creative fashion?

Modern physics as well as Eastern and Western mysticism and American Indian ideology all indicate existence unfolds in an ordered patterned repeating fashion, down to the very molecules, atoms, protons, neutrons, electrons, quarks and anti-quarks. Everything that is in time and space, occurs in patterns that repeat. With Facticity, we create the environment and the space to explore and discover for ourselves whether this is accurate and/or relevant to living a better life.

Notes:

Chapter 6

Acceptance and Presence — Keys Unlocking the Door of Now

". . . Sometime again soon, no hello, no good-bye — all the time Here . . ."
Eskimo Salutation

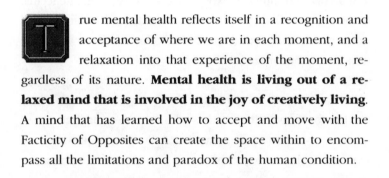rue mental health reflects itself in a recognition and acceptance of where we are in each moment, and a relaxation into that experience of the moment, regardless of its nature. **Mental health is living out of a relaxed mind that is involved in the joy of creatively living**. A mind that has learned how to accept and move with the Facticity of Opposites can create the space within to encompass all the limitations and paradox of the human condition.

We can free the mind to be wholly involved in the joy of creatively living as we shift our way of *relating* to the mind, recognizing it is not who we are. When this is done, freedom comes to actually taste the reality of being more than that mind and more than the body.

Human beings identify with the mind (and its emotions) as who we are.

Facticity

As we come to understand *how* the mind works and can see
and feel and hear it in action, it becomes clearer that we are
not that mind/body experience. For example, even though we
can see and feel our hands, we know it is not who we are. It is
a part of our body, yes, but not the essence of who we are. We
cannot be what we are watching, hearing or feeling, because
we are doing the watching. We cannot be that which we can
see, feel or hear happening *to* us or *within* us.

Because of this deep unconscious identification with the mind
(and its emotions) as who we are, we remain undeveloped in
our ability to distinguish experiential knowing from intellectual
knowing, and frequently feel disconnected from our spiritual
roots which rest beyond mind. Most of us in today's world are
lost in a mental maze with no apparent way out.

With Facticity, we are exploring a way out of the mind, a way
to dis-identify with the mind as who we are, through a natural
ability that we have forgotten. That ability is to be present — to
come to our senses for the actual experience of being alive,
seeing, hearing, feeling, tasting, smelling, touching.

**In the presence of life as a sensory experience,
mind can be delegated to its rightful place as a part
with a part to play, but definitely not the role of
Head Master.**

ven as you continue reading now . . .

your body alive . . .

with the sounds and sensations of life . . .

your unconscious mind can widen that awareness now . . .

and allow that seeing . . . hearing . . .

smelling . . . tasting . . .

feeling of now . . .

can move inside that awareness . . .

inviting you to relax . . .

and learn the feel of just being . . .

right here . . .

and right now . . .

reading these words . . .

allowing the flow of your response to unfold . . .

moment to moment . . .

like the petals of a flower do let go. . .

revealing that hidden beauty and fragrance . . .

your unconscious mind can free that new understanding . . .

beginning to flower . . .

as the sensations of life continue now . . .

yours to enjoy . . .

As human beings, we have many abilities and resources. At least two of these remain generally unused and unavailable in our efforts to create a full life. Through Facticity, we can evoke these powerful capacities and re-educate them to work in new ways.

The first of these is the unconscious mind itself with its abilities to learn and create new behaviors. The unconscious mind knows how to receive an experience, how to grasp it, how to make it clear, how to tune it up, so it can use that experience as a foundation to build and create other experiences. When we had our first childhood experience of standing on our own two feet, all by ourself, the unconscious mind knew how to use that experience to build an unconscious foundation. It then used that learning to go on and build the learnings of how to walk and run and skip and hop, and even discover the intricate experience of dancing.

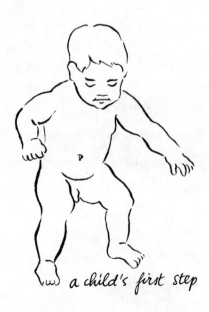

a child's first step

The second is that vast wealth of discounted experiential knowledge we have been gathering from the beginning of life — things we know that we don't know we know. For example, day can't exist without night and up can't exist without down. The brighter a light is, the darker its shadow. And, you can't go out unless you're already in.

Through the Facticity process, we bring these abilities together in a way that frees us to formulate for ourselves new ways to relate to this very uncertain circumstance and experience called living. These new ways to relate will be based on our own personal experience of how life really works, including the discounted experience that up to now has been ignored by the unconscious mind as a possible source of information and support for living fully, graciously and efficiently.

For example, if the unconscious mind considered it relevant that without valleys, there could be no mountain peaks, and without peaks, there could be no valleys, perhaps the way we related to our own highs and lows could shift. Unconscious awareness of the facticity of how peaks and valleys are essential to one another — how they give birth to one another — how they relax with one another — can impact on the experience of our own peaks and valleys.

Your unconscious mind . . .

can gather these remembrances now . . .

for you have traveled many a land . . .

and perhaps climbed many a mountain . . .

enjoyed resting in many a valley . . .

and do you know . . .

without those mountains . . .

there can be no valleys . . .

and without those valleys . . . why . . .

there can be no mountains. . .

and together . . .

the terrain becomes fresh . . .

alive with new kinds of life at every stage of the journey . . .

climbing up that mountain . . .

or climbing down inside the valley . . .

you can free that ability to flow . . .

from the highest peak . . .

brilliant with the light of that height you've reached . . .

sliding with ease and comfort now . . .

right on in . . .

to even the darkest, deepest valley . . .

knowing . . .

the valley needs the mountains to be . . .

the mountains resting in the hands of the valley . . .

and together . . .

the land becomes rich to travel . . .

With Facticity, we are re-educating the unconscious mind to know what it was taught not to know a long time ago, and to pay attention to that vast wealth of personal experience that we continue to gather even now. The unconscious mind can organize that *discounted* experience to support both a new foundation at the unconscious level, and the creation of new ways to relate to the basic facticities of life.

As children, we are basically taught not to know a lot of things. We're taught not to see a lot, not to hear a lot, and not to feel a lot. And in those childhood learnings, a great deal of what we *can* know about how life actually works becomes unavailable. We miss a tremendous amount of the life experience that is really ours to claim. We lose access to a great deal of material that can help us create guidelines for how to actually move in this continually changing and constantly uncertain experience of being alive.

The more we can know what we were taught not to know, the more in touch we become with our own experiential learnings. With this knowledge, it becomes easier to discover *how* to live in harmony with the flow of life.

Chapter 7

Experience — The Best Teacher There Is

". . . The hidden harmony is better than the obvious . . ."
Heraclitus
Greek Mystic

I f we are truly more than the mind/body and some- how a meaningful part of existence, then that reality (commonly called spiritual) must be knowable by us *through experience*. Thinking, contemplating and being philo- sophical puts us *in* the mind itself which is, by its very nature, one step away from the actual experience of living.

Facticity proposes a return to our senses, a coming back to ourselves, as the avenue through which these possibilities can be explored. It is an adventurous exploration of discovering — for ourselves — experiential reality outside the mind.

By coming to our senses, literally experiencing our experience through being *present* for it, we can know that life flows with certain undeniable and unalterable patterns that repeat in an ordered and creative fashion. With that knowledge, we auto- matically create a new way of relating to living that includes the response of balance — a necessary experience for mental health and movement beyond the mind.

*A*nd as your unconscious mind . . .

moves to explore how to rearrange . . .

those old learnings now in new ways . . .

allowing what's been unequal to come into balance . . .

creating the space . . .

to allow the movement of your being . . .

to move into balance now . . .

like that time long ago you might have stood . . .

on the edge of a curb . . .

beginning to experience how it feels to balance on the edge . . .

pretending perhaps the curb is a tightrope . . .

strung high above the earth and you're walking on that thin

line . . .

and a person can feel the balancing begin . . .

as they walk . . .

balancing one foot and then the other . . .

holding the arms out to allow the balance to come . . .

moving to the left, then to the right and back again . . .

back and forth to find that moment of balance . .

that comes and goes . . .

The NLP technology of sub-modalities (see Glossary) provides a potent framework to help us actually come out of the mind and be present for the experience of what is happening beyond the filters of belief, demand, and expectation.

The ability to be present, to be in the "now" and free of effect from the mind's discriminating judgements is one of the desired outcomes of content-free meditation. This type of meditation creates an environment in which something happens that mind cannot do.

The mind cannot provide insight from the realm of our spiritual nature. However, working with mind via meditation creates an environment conducive to insight arising. (One definition of insight is seeing intuitively, or a direct knowing that arises without cognitive thought.)

There are several categories of meditation techniques. One is designed to develop mental concentration, or the capacity of the mind to hold its focus and attention on one point, allowing all else to remain outside awareness. These techniques include mantras, inner visualization, mandalas, chanting and others where our attention is directed to remain on one thing and one thing only to the exclusion of all else.

Another category is designed to invite insight to occur through the development of awareness. In these techniques, the object is to hold our awareness steady and allow everything that arises within it to be there, and to pass away, while we simply watch the flow and allow. Each of these categories is geared to develop different mental capacities. (And there are, of course, teachings that combine both aspects into a single practice.)

Facticity draws on the second category with a content-free technique which is a natural extension of awareness of sub-modalities. (In NLP, sub-modalities are considered to be the universal building blocks of subjective experience. See Glossary.) This process develops the ability to experience what is often called bare attention or awareness of actual sensory experience before the observer's own mind interprets or labels the experience via discriminating thought, projection, or hallucination.

For example, when the experience of blushing is occurring, there exists the basic sensations of heat and movement as the blood vessels open and the blood flows more fully into the face. It is possible to be aware and present for these sensations, experiencing them fully as sensations, *before* the label of blushing arises and the interpretation that it is an embarrassing situation. When this kind of aware presence is available, it can short circuit the impact of old labels and interpretations.

As human beings, we discount most of our experience and go with mental concepts and abstractions instead. We move with these abstractions to the point where we begin to question whether we could ever have the real experience or not.

The real experience of living is right here, available for us to know and existing in that realm right outside the mind.

With Facticity, we are helping ourselves create a map of how to move through the terrain of life more as it really is, *before* we add in the work of the discriminating mind (judgements, values, opinions). We are doing this by coming back to our sensory experience, back to our senses, to what is really verifiable through our eyes and ears and nose and hands and feet and even that inner sense of knowing that some of us call a still, silent voice. To travel through the Himalayas with a map of the Sahara as your guide will bring great confusion and discomfort.

traveling through the himalayas with a map of the desert

The Facticity of Opposites is an experiential reality we all know exists. Yet, this knowledge is discounted because our unconscious presuppositions and assumptions work to keep these knowings outside our awareness. Experience that does not support our basic unconscious assumptions simply isn't noticed. If I unconsciously believe that happiness lies in being married, I will never notice those single people who are happy alone.

nd your unconscious mind can search there . . .

to remember your ability to relax . . .

as you walk through the days of your life . . .

the times of day change . . .

the temperatures change . . .

as the evenings come and go . . .

the phases of the moon change . . .

and it's curious to know . . .

the new moon does its change where it cannot be seen . . .

invisible while the night is dark . . .

the new moon allows its change to occur . . .

easily . . .

deep in the womb of the night . . .

and as you become aware . . .

you can relax with change . . .

you may feel those shifts already begun here . . .

changes that your unconscious mind has allowed . . .

in the rhythm of that breathing . . .

the pulse rate . . .

changing that feeling so you can rest . . .

and allow that relaxation . . .

continuing to come . . .

and free you to recognize . . .

change that is natural and easy now . . .

Personal experience is the highest level of evidence and information that we can gather about how to live life in a way that works. Often times, however, we are only considering a small portion of our experience, and we often have only one way to relate to that experience. Perhaps the way Aunt Jill taught us when we were 10 is the only way we learned as the right way. And more than likely that's the only way our unconscious mind has ever considered possible.

When the unconscious mind realizes this wealth of discounted experience is here and *relevant* to allowing us a fuller, richer, safer, more creative and productive life, it will generally be delighted to go ahead and explore the possibilities of utilizing that information.

As that reservoir of hidden resources continues to be uncovered, the addition of content-free meditation gives the traveler in this journey someplace solid to reside as the mind expands and re-organizes itself to hold the paradox and limitations of life.

It is a curious recognition, then, that the ultimate sense of security seems to rest in accepting insecurity or a constant flow of change, as simply the way life is. When the unconscious mind is free to recognize the Facticity of Opposites (or duality) as the *pattern* of that inevitable flow, a new understanding begins to arise.

For the mind seeking transformation, it becomes clear that change is what we are trying to do to ourselves. It also becomes clear that understanding is something that happens. **And it is known that understanding, not change, is what finally allows transformation to occur.**

Notes:

Chapter 8

Beliefs — The Wonder of Selective Perception

". . . Real harmony is neither to go with nor to go against. Let reality possess you. Just be overwhelmed by that which is inescapable and you will find immense peace . . ."
                                                            Tai Hui
                                                            Zen Master

ecause we are taught not to see, not to hear and not to know so much, we end up spending a great deal of time in our minds thinking *about* life instead of being free to experience it directly. Another outcome of this "learned not-knowing" is the necessity of acquiring beliefs. Since "knowing" is assumed to be unavailable, we are handed beliefs about those things we don't know. We learn to operate out of those beliefs as if they were true.

Because beliefs act as filters, they only let us see what supports the belief — not what challenges it. Beliefs cause us to discount, or not see, many things we can know through experience. Thus, the facticity of many experiences becomes deleted and unavailable for use.

If I believe life is basically a tough experience, I won't notice those times that are simple and easy. At the unconscious level, they will be discounted as irrelevant information and kept from my view and consideration. However, if I believe that life is both difficult and easy, I will be open to both kinds of experiences and have more information available for living with ease.

It is useful to know how to believe and how to make beliefs work for us. However, when a belief solidifies into a truth that is unable to reflect itself in universal experience, it is important to stop and question it. Is this really true or is this something I want to be true?

Beliefs become real for the mind/body system. What we believe to be true can become true physiologically as well. However, when viewed from that point of view outside the mind, beliefs are like a dream — real while being dreamed, but upon awakening, recognized as a creation of mind, an illusion.

Awareness of Facticity allows us to relax with this seeming paradox and remain free to accept illusion as real for the mind/body system, and not-real, or not the final reality, when perceived from that point of view outside the mind.

We are using Facticity to support trust in our *discounted experience*, and making our own choice, our own decision about how to relate to things recognized as unavoidable facticities in the experience of being alive.

Although Facticity has little to do with believing, beliefs are what drive us to act and to move in certain ways. With Facticity, we are re-educating the unconscious mind to recognize where it does not have to move out of beliefs by working with beliefs directly.

There is enough universal experiential information available (things we can know) to free us to live harmoniously with life.

*A*nd your unconscious mind . . .

can continue now . . .

sorting through that experience unnoticed before . . .

setting aside those old beliefs . . .

that you can recognize now are no longer needed . . .

as you continue discovering . . .

the value of that experience . . .

set aside in the past . . .

now moving forward . . .

to be seen and heard and felt . . .

that powerful source of learning now . . .

what you were taught not to know then . . .

is yours now . . .

isn't it? . . .

It seems absurd to throw away any experience before totally and thoroughly exploring it as a possible source of information. Believing has its place, its part and its power. However, there is another level where "what is" takes the forefront.

Imagine for a moment that you're climbing a mountain and you enter the Land of Belief. Here is the realm of imagination and powers of the mind. Here is great space for discovering and harnessing the abilities of mind to create and manifest. So, you travel through this terrain, learning, exploring, and getting the gist of creating your own reality.

mount metaphor

Then, one day, perhaps without even knowing, you find yourself beyond the border of the Land of Belief and inside the Realm of What Is. You try and try to make things happen here as you succeeded in doing before, but somehow it isn't working. In the Realm of What Is something new is needed, something in addition to powers of mind. This is the terrain where Facticity becomes of great value. Belief will be of use in this Realm as well, but the keys of passage through this land are acceptance and presence.

Through Facticity, we have the time and the guidance to separate beliefs from experience and then use those appropriate experiential learnings to relate to life in whatever new way will make the most sense to us — as we are now — with all our years of experience in being alive.

Knowing the power of beliefs, Facticity helps us pinpoint blocking beliefs and change them. We can utilize the power of belief by creating new beliefs that are not only positive, and process oriented, but also inclusive of the Facticity of Opposites and a new way to relate to whatever opposite has been denied, ignored, or de-valued by the original belief.

For example, I might have an old belief that I am stupid. Becoming aware that stupidity and intelligence are but two ends of a single process that moves from one point to the other again and again, I might want to revise my belief to allow myself less stress and more acceptance when the moments of stupidity or ignorance arise. My new belief might sound something like — I believe I am learning to recognize my moments of intelligence as well as my moments of stupidity, welcoming those times of feeling stupid as safeguarding my intelligence, inviting me to remain alert and open to new information, input, and things I don't yet know through my own experience and understanding.

And the unconscious mind . . .

can draw on the power . . .

of your un-noticed experience now . . .

creating new ways . . .

to relate to life . . .

to be aware you can flow with that pressure . . .

you can allow that pain to guide you back to yourself . . .

as you watch . . .

exploring . . . becoming aware . . .

that you are . . .

alive . . .

dancing in this flow of endings and beginnings . . .

lightness and shadows . . .

like the very air you breathe . . .

right here . . . right now . . .

coming in and going out . . .

and your unconscious mind can . . .

allow this unfolding . . .

returning into your awareness . . .

what you were taught not to know . . .

only as fast or as slow . . .

as is just right for you . . .

can trust your experience . . .

to guide you now . . .

as you go ahead and step out of those old beliefs . . .

you know you're ready to let go of . . .

and invite your unconscious mind . . .

to ground you in that new trust . . .

taking root in your experience now . . .

revealing to you life's patterns . . .

that are yours to know . . .

When we allow Opposites to exist as they are, free to continue in their flow back and forth, each extreme valued in its own right, a new kind of understanding begins to arise. If I believe I am ugly, I will begin to recognize my beauty must be here as well. One cannot exist without the other. If I believe I am stupid, I will begin to recognize my intelligence must be here too. One cannot exist without the other. A new relaxation begins to arise and the ability to accept whatever experience is occurring becomes easier and stronger.

Chapter 9

Consciously Creating Useful Illusions

". . . When no discriminating thoughts arise, the old mind ceases to exist . . ."

Sengsten
Third Zen Patriarch

eliefs are basically what drive our behaviors and are very powerful motivators. However, beliefs are often the very thing blocking our ability to experience life in new ways.

We are using Facticity to re-educate the unconscious mind to the presence and relevance of our discounted experience, and to work with creating new beliefs that will work in our favor. We can harness the power of beliefs and use that power to propel ourselves towards choiceless awareness or non-judgemental acceptance of all that we are.

The difficulty with positive thinking and affirmations as they exist right now is the general denial of the reality of Opposites. And this denial eventually puts us right back where we started. With the Facticities of Change and Opposites, it is inevitable that the unwanted state will arise again — perhaps in another form, but its essence of being in opposition to the desired experience remains. Remember, if we're already in the Realm of What Is, if we've journeyed that far already, new guidelines for travel are required.

the keys of acceptance and presence

Facticity works to expand our beliefs to incorporate whatever facticity is being denied — to embrace it and allow it its rightful place as part of the fabric of life for the mind/body to explore.

As human beings, we all have an innate desire to connect with our "spiritual" self. We may respond differently to that desire, but it is there in all of us. Sooner or later, we all awaken in the middle of the night wondering just why we are here and what this experience is all about.

As we follow that desire to "know" and to "connect" and allow it to pull us toward that third aspect of the body/mind/spirit triad, we inevitably run directly into our minds. In fact, many spiritual explorers perceive mind as the enemy of meditation and the enemy of living in the now.

However, with the advent of NLP and Ericksonian Hypnosis, we have technologies available to use the mind to expand the experience of consciousness, and to move beyond the mind itself. With this exploration are coming many useful learnings about mental health, and how to create that state of living out of a relaxed mind involved in the joy of creatively living.

Recognizing the need for unconscious recognition of the Facticity of Opposites is an enormous leap in this process of evoking mental and emotional balance.

nd sometimes a person can forget to
remember the body's wisdom . . .
that knows the beauty and power . . .
of allowing that positive and that negative to flow together . . .
to work together . . .
deep on the inside . . .
its very cells . . .
the wondrous pull between that positive and that negative force . . .
those seeming opposites . . .

yet very natural connection between the positive and the negative . . .

allowing those cells to stay together . . .

freeing that body to move . . .

to discover all that it can be . . .

that's right . . .

at the heart of the matter . . .

for the opposite of right . . .

isn't always wrong . . .

because what's left to do now . . .

is go ahead and learn from that body's wisdom . . .

and allow those old beliefs to shift and change now . . .

allowing in what's been kept out before . . .

as the unconscious mind builds that new . . .

solidly flexible unconscious foundation . . .

right on that discounted experience . . .

that is yours to draw upon . . .

now . . .

Hypnosis and NLP are powerful tools for change. Facticity uses these tools to reshape the structure and the psychology of the mind from a barrier into a bridge beyond mind. The bridge is built through the recognition and acceptance of Opposites, and the capacity to move in sensory experience. As this occurs, we can more easily balance in our minds and become free to step outside of them into that place beyond mind — whether called

No-Mind, Samadhi, Christ Consciousness, Enlightenment, Nirvana, Self-Realization or one of a dozen other fingers pointing to the moon.

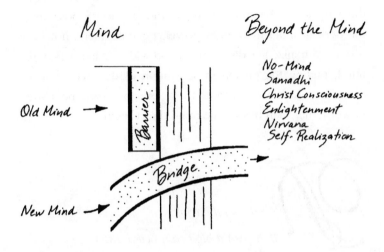

Imagine a coin and remember the mind thinks of a coin as being two-sided. However, there is a third side and that is the rim. When viewing the coin from that third perspective, both sides are available for viewing, and more importantly, they are both *below* you. Identification with either side leads to imbalance. Dis-identification, or distance, from both sides allows balance and a different perspective to become available. Please be aware that dis-identification does not mean dissociation or closing down feeling. Dis-identification and feeling can and do occur simultaneously, although they do not have to.

It is interesting that many mystics indicate the main difference between madness and enlightenment is, in fact, *perspective* in relationship to mind.

Madness has been described as complete identification with the activities of the mind (thoughts and emotions), positioning the person under the mind's power. Enlightenment, however, is often verbalized as dis-identification with the activities of the mind, putting the person in a position of distance from the thoughts and emotions, and thus able to direct the mind's power rather than having the mind direct them.

nd isn't it curious . . .

that even a big heavy ocean liner . . .

might resist the directions to change direction . . .

and keep right on going maybe a mile or more . . .

the way it no longer needs to go . . .

even after the rudder goes down in the water . . .

and the new directions have been given . . .

yet a captain who knows his ship . . .

allows that time . . .

to resist that change of course . . .

knowing full well when that resistance has run its course . . .

the new direction will take hold . . .

and that knowing . . .

can cause the unconscious mind now . . .

to locate those old beliefs you're ready to leave behind . . .

and use your own experience . . .

easily and more intensely now . . .

uncovering that new direction . . .

of your choice . . .

Chapter 10

The Unconscious Mind — Our Source of Permission for Change

". . . Just let things be in their own way, and there will be neither coming nor going . . ."

Sengsten
Third Zen Patriarch

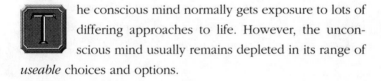he conscious mind normally gets exposure to lots of differing approaches to life. However, the unconscious mind usually remains depleted in its range of *useable* choices and options.

The unconscious mind is quite capable of picking up and utilizing what the conscious mind has learned. However, the unconscious mind is dedicated to protecting us and needs to be absolutely certain what we want to be doing is in our own best interest. The unconscious mind makes this decision based upon existing beliefs, presuppositions and assumptions about how to live life rightly.

It is commonly assumed that conscious understanding of an unwanted pattern will produce behavioral change. However, experience is telling us otherwise. Too many of us can explain exactly why we are so messed up and unhappy, where it began, who was involved, and what misunderstanding or misperception got installed at the time. However, we still find ourselves reacting with basically the same unwanted behavioral responses.

Dr. Milton Erickson recognized that conscious insight did not always produce behavioral change. His pioneering work in the field of hypnosis has left us a vast array of new techniques and new understandings of the power and workings of the unconscious mind — and our need to work with it *directly*.

The unconscious mind has access to all of our experience and the ability to use that experience. However, it may not have a useful way to relate to that experience or perceive it as relevant. That's where we use Facticity to begin the re-education process. New alternatives are offered for consideration via the use of truisms and metaphor in pleasantly altered states of consciousness (see *Lions In Wait*).

Once the unconscious mind becomes aware that certain patterns exist and are relevant, it can reorganize and reassociate its experiences according to those patterns, incorporating their presence in a useful manner. The unconscious mind can build a wholly new, solid, yet flexible unconscious foundation allowing us to move and flow with the fundamental facticities in a much more relaxed and comfortable way.

The basic fabric of life isn't going to change. It is what it is. However, recognizing there is an order and pattern to the way life moves that we can *experience for ourselves*, opens the door to a whole new understanding of mental health and a whole new way of being ourselves comfortably.

We can come to our life experiences with a fresh perspective, open to grasping another way to feel about life, and, for perhaps the first time, free to tune in and hear what nature, both outside and inside the body, is saying about living harmoniously.

nd your unconscious mind can learn . . .

from your experience . . .

of the trees . . . of the wind . . .

your experience of the sky that remains boundless . . .

expansive behind the clouds . . .

continuing to use those knowings now . . .

to allow your energies to flow . . .

naturally . . .

like the waters of a river flow . . .

from the left bank to the right . . .

without concern . . .

allowing that flow . . .

from one side to the other . . .

as the river bed carries the water . . .

on its way . . .

continuing its journey . . .

of returning to that source . . .

To free the unconscious mind to align all its powers and abilities toward this direction of full self-acceptance, hidden beliefs and presuppositions must be pinpointed and challenged. What stops us from making the changes we want right now can be a variety of things. For most, however, a pattern of behavior will have its roots in an unconscious presupposition (belief or assumption).

Almost all the beliefs and assumptions we have are rooted in deeply hidden presuppositions that deny the value and the acceptance of almost half of the experiences life seems to insist we have. The following are some common ones.

1. Security is possible (a place where no change will occur).

2. Death is escapable (somehow).

3. Death is a one-time experience to be fought against.

4. The way to get rid of pain and pressure is to be against them (to avoid them) and to be for pleasure and comfort.

5. There does exist a "right" way to move in the world that can make me happy.

6. Intellectual knowledge is more valuable than experiential knowledge.

7. Others know something I don't. Trust others before trusting myself.

8. Life is logical.

9. Acquisition equals happiness (whether it be beauty, health, comfort, money, material items, love, approval, respect, awareness, enlightenment, etc.).

10. The ego (that sense of self as different and separate) needs to be defended and protected.

11. Others are more valuable and important than I am. I am worthless and of little importance or value.

12. In order to be really good, loving and open, I can never be bad, hateful or closed.

In language, a presupposition is a sentence that has to be true in order for another sentence to make sense. For example, if I say, "The peacocks ate the roses in the Master's garden", we have to presuppose as true that there are peacocks, roses, a Master, a garden, that the garden belongs to the Master, that peacocks eat roses, and both roses and peacocks were in the garden together.

peacocks eating roses in a garden

Presuppositions generally rest outside the realm of conscious attention and are not immediately available for conscious consideration. For this reason, the actual validity of most presuppositions is never questioned.

We simply *assume* the truth, unconsciously, in order to make sense out of what is being said. This is very useful when the presupposition or belief supports, for example, the existence of confidence, courage, or trust in our capacities to move beyond survival to create a full and satisfying life. It can rest there, outside of awareness, and free the conscious mind to attend to the joys of living.

However, hidden presuppositions (or beliefs) that support the distortion or deletion of valuable experience and information become a major source of human dis-ease.

Through Facticity, we can uncover these hidden presuppositions, beliefs and values and work to realign them with our current knowledge and information, including our up-to-now discounted experience and awareness of how the Facticity of Opposites affects all these ideas and assumptions about life.

And your unconscious mind . . .

can continue this exploration . . .

in just the right way for you . . .

because some things you thought you could never do . . .

can happen . . .

in ways you might never have known . . .

it's possible to move in a whole new way . . .

with a lightness that can even feel like soaring . . .

allowing the rainbow of your feelings . . .

free to show their colors . . .

and dance their dance . . .

blossoming in just your way . . .

and within every seed . . .

the blossom rests hidden . . .

unmanifest . . . invisible to the eye . . .

and you can know in every experience . . .

rests the seed . . .

of its other side . . .

and with that knowing . . .

you can continue . . .

relaxing now . . .

and trusting your abilities . . .

to move with life . . .

to flow like the rivers water . . .

back and forth . . .

in and round all that comes in its way . . .

continuing now on your journey . . .

inviting that unconscious mind . . .

to create new behaviors that can free you . . .

to relax with change . . .

to dance with opposites . . .

allowing the circles to complete . . .

relaxing in the beginning of the end . . .

and the end of each beginning . . .

If it is possible to really create a life without suffering (pain because of the pain), then that creation can arise more easily through understanding and relaxing with our patterns of mind and the pattern of Opposites so delicately woven inside the very experience of living.

Notes:

Chapter 11

Trust — A 'Learned Inability'

". . . Great knowledge sees all in one. Small knowledge breaks down into the many . . ."

The Way of Chuang Tzu
Thomas Merton

ne of the hardest things for most of us to do is trust ourselves and our experience. Much of this "learned inability" is because the unconscious mind has not been educated to trust itself or to know itself. We have almost all been taught to look outside of ourselves for verification that we are right, OK, or even on the right track. How many times have we asked another if we look alright, if what we said was OK, or if what we're feeling is reasonable or justified.

Accepting this pre-programmed perspective of the unconscious mind, Facticity helps us look first outside of ourselves, to nature and the rest of existence. Then, we slowly move back inside ourselves using awareness of the miracles without as probable reflections of miracles within.

The tiny seed's display of courage when it follows that inner desire to become more than a seed, sprouting those rootlets and leaving being a seed behind, could become a support for easier letting go. The migrating bird's incredible willingness to follow some unknown pull from the inside, leading to a destination unknown, could influence us to trust our inner knowings more easily.

As the fundamental facticities become verified by our up-to-now discounted experience, we also become aware the rest of existence has its own ways of relating to these facticities that apparently work — perhaps even better than our way which, up to now, has been choosing what we like over what we dislike. With this new information, the unconscious mind can create guidelines for how to relate to these facticities differently.

To move from believing to exploring the possibilities of know-ing requires trust — trust in our own experience — trust that the knowing being sought is available through experience — trust that as human beings we have all that we need to be able to move with life as it really is — trust that there is a process and we are in it. When we experience the fundamental factici-ties again and again and again, a trust begins to develop in that ordered and creative patterning, and in the existence of a process of which we are a part.

Beliefs presuppose certain things as true that we, in fact, do not know for certain. That is the nature of believing. These presup-positions act as filters on our experience and cause us to see only what we want to see.

True trust differs in that it rests solely on experiential knowings *up to the present moment in time.* Thus, the resulting presuppo-sitions include *no guarantee* for how the future will have to unfold. It only implies that it will probably unfold in an ordered and patterned manner as has the past, but recognizes that it might not. We simply cannot know for sure. Thus, we remain free to explore *all* our experience for useful learnings. This allows the mind to open to the experience of the present with a whole new attitude for exploration and learning.

nd how curious those birds know . . .

that inner feeling . . .

that inner pull . . .

to go ahead and make that flight . . .

leaving behind what is known . . .

traveling to a destination not yet seen . . .

invisible yet felt . . .

and those birds simply follow that inner knowing . . .

that it's time to soar high . . .

and fly to new terrain never experienced before . . .

and the unconscious mind can recognize . . .

those experiences that are your experiences . . .

allowing that awareness of your own knowings . . .

to continue arising now . . .

as the unconscious mind . . .

uses those now noticed times of learning . . .

to go on . . .

and create that courage and clarity to travel on . . .

wherever the pull may take you . . .

trusting that wealth of knowing . . .

you can relax now . . .

and trust your ability to move forward . . .

and learn . . .

The experiencing of these fundamental facticities continuing to demonstrate their presence throughout existence can strengthen our inner willingness to explore going with life as it is — to discover our own abilities to flow with the way life actually moves. Fighting with life hasn't worked. Facticity is for those who would like to explore another way — for those who would like to nourish that seed of trust that life is a process and we are a part of the process unfolding.

trusting the flow of life

The unconscious mind must be convinced that it is appropriate and useful to trust itself and make use of the experience it already has.

When the unconscious mind receives information that is impactful enough and powerful enough, our projected outcomes will be accepted and shifts in relating can occur.

Because we are all unique, the way in which these shifts occur will also be unique. It is important to remember there is no specific way in which these shifts in relating have to happen — other than happening in a way that is unique to you — your own way.

nd as you begin to recognize now . . .

you are you . . .

seemingly the same, seemingly different . . .

and people are both alike . . .

and different . . .

and it's all right . . .

to be yourself comfortably . . .

moving with the flow of moving yourself . . .

to recognize that uniqueness . . .

because after all human beings have two eyes and a nose . . .

two ears and a mouth . . .

a forehead and cheeks and a chin . . .

but there's no other combination . . .

exactly like yours . . .

and that makes your face unique . . .

and it's just that uniqueness . . .

all those things you like and dislike . . .

that makes you, you . . .

and your unconscious mind . . .

can lay the foundations now . . .

to recognize that uniqueness . . .

to respect that . . .

one and only expression of life . . .

to begin to feel . . .

a good feeling . . .

knowing . . .

there's only one of you . . .

and perhaps . . .

existence wants you . . .

to allow that uniqueness to emerge . . .

blossoming fully . . .

allowing that fragrance . . .

that is uniquely yours . . .

to dance with the wind . . .

and it's nice to remember . . .

everything blooms in its own time . . .

and your unconscious mind . . .

can take all the time it needs . . .

to sort through those experience that are yours now . . .

to bring forth those guidelines . . .

that can free you to see yourself in a new light . . .

listen to yourself with a new ear . . .

feel yourself with a new sense . . .

because you are unique . . .

in all the world . . .

and there's nothing can be done about that . . .

The way we relate to fundamental facticities is at the root of easy living or living with dis-ease.

We are unaware that we have the strengths and capacities to do more than cope. We don't know we have what we need to be with life as it is. As we become aware of these strengths and abilities, we learn to trust *our* way of moving will arise naturally from within. How that will be specifically must remain unknown until it arrives. Each of us is an individual and can learn to trust our natural ability to express that uniqueness in our own creative fashion.

(See *Lions In Wait.* Chapter #7 — A Tree Of Trust demonstrates how hypnosis can be utilized to evoke this shift toward trusting ourselves, our process, and our experience by skillfully and elegantly challenging the truth of certain hidden assumptions presupposed to be true via the evocation and presentation of undeniably true experience.)

Chapter 12

Separating Realities — Body/Mind and Spirit

". . . The waking have one world in common; sleepers have each a private world of his own . . ."

Heraclitus
Greek Mystic

M ost of us accept the idea that our human nature consists of a body, mind and spirit. These three aspects, although intimately connected and related, produce different categories of experience and perception. The spirit aspect, in particular, has always been thought to be a totally different realm or dimension of our nature, discontinuous, yet not disconnected, with the experience of the body and the mind.

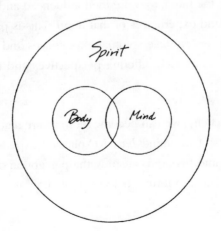

Most of us, at one time or another, have experiences we could describe as spiritual. And it is only human nature to then attempt to bring the experience back into the realm of the mind in order to share or remember by encoding it in our memory and creating a re-presentation of it in the privacy of the mind.

However, experience and perception from the spirit aspect simply doesn't fit into the ability of mind to grasp or hold without distorting that experience or perception in some fashion. Most of us have had experiences that were simply beyond words and no matter what we do, words fail to capture what we experienced and wish to communicate.

Facticity has its roots in the study of spiritual seekers and their patterns of response. Mystics continually indicate that "oneness" is the ultimate reality and "duality" is the reality of the mind/body system.

NLP offers a model of how *subjective* experience is created. From the NLP perspective, once our spiritual experiences are fed through the mind, they are then influenced and colored by the beliefs and experiences of that mind. This is partially why so many of us can have spiritual experiences and then speak about them from such differing perspectives and understandings.

Through Facticity, we can become more aware that the unconscious filters of the mind *have* to split any experience of the mind/body into two, thus creating the perception of duality or Opposites. This can further help to clarify confusions that arise

when we attempt to re-present, through the mind, an experience that we know, in fact, was of "oneness", and all the mind
can reproduce is something quite lacking.

The age old traditions of gurus, Zen Masters and sages sitting in
silence, creating situations that will throw the spiritual seeker
outside the mind, take on a new kind of sense in light of these
more scientific recognitions of *how* the mind works. A certain
kind of relaxation arises once we realize no matter what
knowing of oneness, connectedness, nothingness we have in
the dimension of spirit, it is doomed to be re-presented as two-
ness (duality) when it enters the realm of mind (words, visions,
thoughts and emotion). Hence, the almost universal mystical
reference to silence as a major avenue for travel through and
beyond the mind.

nd as you continue reading these words . . .

an awareness can arise . . .

of the space that invites the formation . . .

of the letters to take shape . . .

the emptiness that allows the fullness to arise . . .

of that meaning becoming clearer . . .

easier to grasp . . .

as the silence behind the sounds . . .

becomes free to speak in a new voice . . .

its pulsing rhythm . . .

felt like the depths of the sea . . .

silent and calm . . . allowing each wave to arise . . .

fresh and new . . .

a part of the sea yet a part set apart for awhile . . .

and your unconscious mind can recognize now . . .

the wave belongs to the sea . . .

even as the sounds belong to the silence . .

NLP offers a valuable and useful model of mind that can help the seeker of both spiritual knowing and mental health. In studying human subjectivity, Richard Bandler, John Grinder, Robert Dilts and others have uncovered certain patterns and processes that are continually in action at the unconscious level of the mind. And it is these unconscious processes that take each of our experiences and make them uniquely our own.

NLP distinguishes between the map and the territory and it is a very valid and important recognition. The map we pull out of our car glove compartment is clearly not the actual territory we intend to travel. It is, instead, a set of guidelines and landmarks to help us travel with greater ease and a sense of knowing where we're going.

Likewise, each of us has a mental map of how to travel through this terrain of living, and that map is not the actual territory of life. The direct experience of the territory cannot be obtained through the map. We can use the map to guide us, but a traveler can easily see the territory is quite different from those lines and marks on that paper.

the map is not the reality

Facticity recognizes that when we step into the spirit aspect of our nature, the territory becomes available for direct experiencing. Just as travelers can shift their attention from the map to the actual land being covered, seekers of spiritual knowing and mental health can learn to shift their attention from their mental map of beliefs and opinions to the ability to directly experience the journey as it unfolds through the presence of sensory experience.

This focusing of attention is brought under conscious control and strengthened via meditation. We can then shift our attention from certain non-useful or non-skillful mind/body reactions and perceptions, and create space for higher levels of perception to emerge — perceptions that can become the foundation for walking on out of the mind into other dimensions of our nature.

The ability to "put aside" the mind and emotions (personality) in a healthy way, making space for higher level perceptions to arise, is developed by recognizing our own patterns of mind and shifting our attention away from them to sensory experience of the moment.

nd it's curious to become aware . . .

the center of a cyclone is always calm . . .

the center untouched by the raging forces of the winds . . .

furious in their movement . . .

and the center moves with the storm . . .

as it arises, the center is there . . .

as it unfolds in its fury and movement, the center is there . . .

calm . . . untouched . . .

and as the storm dies . . .

the center remains . . . to receive the winds . . .

as they dissolve into the waiting arms . . .

of the atmosphere . . .

always there . . .

as your awareness awaits like a calm, center of a storm . . .

after the cyclone dispells itself . . .

into the very sky . . .

the center remains . . .

like the ocean itself . . .

salty in the center . . .

salty on the shores . . .

for wherever the ocean is . . .

as it surrounds, envelopes and engulfs the life that swims in

the sea . . .

the taste is salty everywhere . . .

and do you suppose the fish . . .

that live in the sea . . .

are thirsty? . . .

or are they aware . . .

of that very environment which is their home . . .

supporting and nourishing them . . .

through every moment of their life there . . .

Many seekers report confusion, and even despair, at the continuing presence of thoughts and feelings considered to be barriers to enlightenment. They are misperceiving this continuing mental and emotional traffic back and forth between the extremes as a marker of their lack of progress rather than the natural state of the mind. This perception will naturally bring confusion and/or despair, with the seeker somehow forgetting that the realm of the spirit being sought is beyond the mind — not resting within it.

Most maps of meditation hold that a quiet or silent mind is a prerequisite for reaching the desired state. Thus, we generally presuppose that quiet or silence must arise by getting rid of all thought — especially bad thought — rather than presupposing a silence that arises by letting things be as they are — including the mind itself.

If it is not possible to stop the mind by getting rid of bad thoughts and cultivating good ones (due to the mechanisms of mind and the Facticities of Change and Opposites), then perhaps simply relaxing into the flow of both kinds of thought will produce the desired results. (Content-free meditation does in fact increase the perception of a slowed down mind, or it may be that the distance gained by the meditation practice simply allows the perception of the process speed to change.)

Our personal spiritual maps, the questions we ask and the answers unconsciously seeded inside, are at the foundation of the way we perceive and respond to almost everything else in life. If we wish to transform ourselves and our world, it is only reasonable we become aware of how we perceive our spiritual nature and our spiritual insights. As we explore the use of NLP and Ericksonian Hypnosis to expand awareness of the Facticity of Opposites, we have the opportunity to train our minds in the service of our Being's deepest knowings.

Notes:

Chapter 13

Gestalt Duality — Now You See It, Now You Don't

". . . In a gestalt duality, you can never see both worlds together; if you choose to see one, you have to forget about the other . . ."
Om Mani Padma Hum
Osho

ur Western way of thought is based on Aristotelian logic which says A can only be A and cannot be B, and B can only be B and cannot be A. In other words, A is either A or B, but cannot be both. The Eastern way of thought says A cannot only be A, it can also be B, or A can be both A and B. This is, for the Western mind, generally a great stretch. However, with Facticity, we are working to install just that perception as a new choice.

You may remember the pictures on the next page illustrating certain elements of visual perception. As you stare at them, the Gestalt changes and the picture you see changes. In number one, you may first see an old hag or a beautiful young woman. As you continue looking, the background shifts to the fore-ground and the opposite image arises. No matter how hard you try, you cannot see both the old hag and the beautiful girl simultaneously because *they are made of the same lines in different relationship.*

In number two, you may first see two faces looking at each other, or a vase. As you continue looking, the background shifts to the foreground (or the foreground shifts to the background), and the other image arises. Again, no matter how hard you try, you cannot see both the two faces and the vase at the same time. Each perception gives birth to the other. Each perception rests hidden in the other even as it manifests.

hag or beautiful girl?   *vase or faces?*

This experience reflects the most basic dilemma of being human. We know that both dimensions of our nature are there (spiritual and material, inner and outer), yet we seem intrinsically unable to experience both simultaneously and somehow forced to choose one over the other.

However, when the unconscious mind is operating out of a new choice that allows both to be there, with no preference for either one over the other, we can sit and watch the pictures shift and change, in their own time, in their own way, with no effort and no tension to keep only one of the images in the foreground. An easy flow naturally occurs demonstrating right here the Facticity of Opposites. What was foreground is now background. What was background is now foreground. And you, the one watching, know this process will go on and on, so you can simply relax with it.

nd even the pendulum on an old

grandfather clock . . .

knows as it swings way over to that one side . . .

moving and gathering the momentum as it swings . . .

to` use that momentum . . .

the moment the pendulum reaches that extreme . . .

to let go . . .

and move easily to that other side . . .

and even as the energy dissipates . . .

that was gathered to carry that motion back . . .

to the other side . . .

a new energy is gathering . . .

that can carry that pendulum back yet again . . .

allowing the swing towards completion . . .

to continue moving . . .

dancing its dance . . .

like the tides rolling in . . .

rolling out . . .

a cycle . . .

where one side depends on the other . . .

allowing its existence to rest poised in the womb of what is . . .

the opposite beginning to take shape . . .

and although there are many days . . .

when it seems like night will never come . . .

the cycle goes on . . .

the circle . . .

completing itself yet again and again . . .

With Facticity, we are utilizing the basic Direction Filter of the mind to propel us toward acceptance of *all* we perceive ourselves to be, both good and bad, both awake and asleep, both kind and cruel, both loving and hateful, both beautiful and ugly, both together and alone. We are moving the whole pattern of our thinking out of an "Either/Or" pattern into a new pattern of response which allows us to be "Both/And". To be everything we are, without having to choose or prefer one expression over another, allows us to finally accept ourself in every moment and truly explore the transforming power of self-acceptance and love.

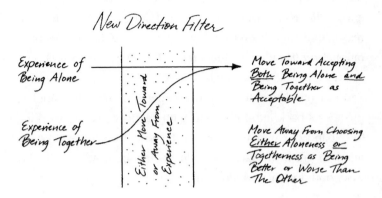

New Direction Filter

Experience of Being Alone → Move Toward Accepting <u>Both</u> Being Alone <u>and</u> Being Together as Acceptable

Experience of Being Together → Either Move Toward or Away From Experience / Move Away From Choosing <u>Either</u> Aloneness <u>or</u> Togetherness as Being Better or Worse Than The Other

Once the unconscious mind, using its innate intelligence and sensitivity, recognizes the value of relaxing in the presence of Opposites (since they are an intrinsic part of the fabric of life), it can shift its guidelines for action and response:

from conscience towards consciousness

from logic towards reasonableness

from beliefs towards experience

If conscience is that set of teachings we received from Mom and Dad and the relatives, ministers and teachers, and consciousness is that natural state of awareness arising when we balance at our center point, the unconscious mind will begin to recognize that consciousness provides more space and clarity out of which to act and respond.

As the unconscious mind begins to accept that every experience in life is *not* logical and rational, it becomes clearly more
reasonable (and therefore logical) to allow life to be both
rational *and* irrational. General conditioning is that life should
always make sense — logical sense. When our conditioning
and our mind tries to force our experience into this mold, it
pushes us back into Either/Or. With Facticity, we are working
to expand our understanding at the *unconscious* level of the
mind to grasp the facticity of life being Both/And — in this
case, both logical and illogical.

When enough discounted experiential knowledge is gathered
together that challenges the unwanted old beliefs, its very
presence will disrupt the power of the old beliefs and cause
new responses to arise.

The human dilemma rests in our reality of having an outer
world and an inner world — or a mind/body and a spirit (soul,
consciousness). Due to what we now know is the biologically
essential Direction Filter of the mind, we are unconsciously
continually choosing one over the other. Traditionally, Western
societies have definitely chosen the outer over the inner and
Eastern societies chosen the inner over the outer, leaving each
suffering from a gross imbalance.

With the recognition of Opposites, it seems clear that acceptance and validation of both is necessary, and a discovering of
how these seemingly opposed realities are in fact complementary and supportive of one another.

The need to balance the spiritual and the material aspects of our nature is obvious, as we watch ourselves and our world crying out in desperation. Yet, until the unconscious mind is re-educated and shifts *away* from choosing one over the other *toward* a choiceless acceptance of both, we will continue to engage in a losing battle of setting up what we like against what we dislike.

nd how nice to know balance . . .

can continue . . .

and your unconscious mind knows . . .

opposites attract . . .

and the balancing begins . . .

allowing the movement that's natural to be . . .

like a juggler juggling . . .

and once a juggler understands the power of his ability . . .

to use a vision that he'd perhaps not known was his own . . .

that peripheral vision allowing movement to be seen . . .

why then a person can look straight ahead . . .

and learn from the movement . . .

seeing its presence . . .

allowing it to be . . .

learning how to hold the balls in the hand . . .

allowing them to change from one hand to another . . .

moving in a rhythm . . .

and once the rhythm of that juggling is felt . . .

why a person can remain in balance with those balls . . .

with that constant flow of movement and motion . . .

as you remain balanced in the middle . . .

like the center of a storm . . .

calm and quietly there . . .

allowing what is to be . . .

The challenge of our day remains discovering *how* to bring the knowings, insights, and needs of our spiritual nature to work side by side and in balance with the knowledge, experience, and needs of our material nature. It seems the new Humane Being will have to transcend biology, and invite new levels of perception to become our guide for the future.

As children, we demonstrate our innate intelligence and sensitivity by shaping our personalities and habits in accordance with our need to survive. Each of us manages to adapt to our childhood environment, and even if the patterns adopted are unhealthy or even seemingly unnatural, retrospect reveals they were the intelligent choice at the time.

When the unconscious mind recognizes that Opposites is the most basic pattern in the fabric of life, it will respond with intelligence and sensitivity, and at the highest level, transformation of our consciousness itself.

Notes:

Chapter 14

Linguistic Loopholes And Language Limitations

". . . Consider movement stationary and the stationary in motion, and both the state of movement and the state of rest disappear . . ."

Sengsten
3rd Zen Patriarch

anguage itself plays a large role in continuing the mind/body experience of duality. In fact, it is linguistically impossible to communicate anything without unconsciously evoking the mechanism of comparison, and comparison presupposes the existence of things being different. Light has no meaning without referencing dark. Up has no meaning without referencing down. Heaven has no meaning without referencing hell.

The mind, in fact, does reference both extremes, but currently relates to them from an Either/Or perspective causing a choice to be made. With Facticity, we are working to change that relationship to an acceptance of both so that choicelessness becomes an option, and with it, a whole new range of possible responses.

Our objective is to offer the mind the new choice of choiceless-ness. We can utilize the propelling power of the mind's Direction Filter from simply moving us toward an experience or away from an experience to moving us toward the specific experience of accepting both, and moving us away from the specific experience of choosing either one or the other.

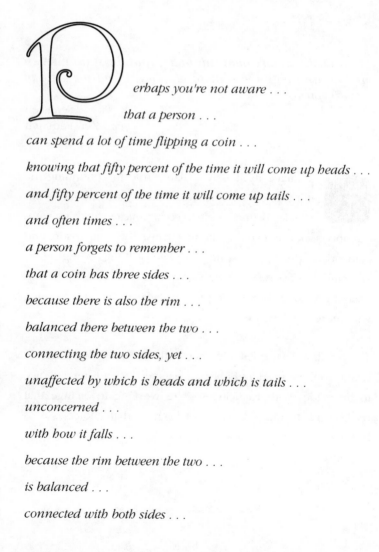

erhaps you're not aware . . .

that a person . . .

can spend a lot of time flipping a coin . . .

knowing that fifty percent of the time it will come up heads . . .

and fifty percent of the time it will come up tails . . .

and often times . . .

a person forgets to remember . . .

that a coin has three sides . . .

because there is also the rim . . .

balanced there between the two . . .

connecting the two sides, yet . . .

unaffected by which is heads and which is tails . . .

unconcerned . . .

with how it falls . . .

because the rim between the two . . .

is balanced . . .

connected with both sides . . .

yet free . . .

to remain itself . . .

to remain free . . .

of that game of heads and tails . . .

yet always present for the play . . .

Phrases like "fighting for peace", "a soldier of God", "demand for peace", "struggling for surrender" reflect our unconscious process denying the Facticity of Opposites as a permanent and unchanging pattern *when life is experienced through the mind.*

Just as language perpetuates the creation of the experience of duality, it can also help create our new option. A hypnotic technique known as the Apposition of Opposites serves as a model. Speaking of a cool warmth, a cold heat, a moving stillness, a heightened depth, a numbing touch, a blinding vision, a bright dimness, a screaming quiet, a loud silence, a silent voice — each of these seemingly opposing experiences presented together forces the mind into moments of confusion for it normally does not organize opposite experiences in this manner.

Use of these linguistic loopholes throughout the Facticity process begins to install this new option by bringing seeming opposites together in the same experiential description. Embedding these confusions inside a context of exploring complementariness and acceptance as a new psychological point of view, increases the probability of the unconscious mind reorganizing and redirecting its energies toward this new option.

It is known that a basic neurological mechanism built in the very structure of the nervous system is balance between opposing systems (Kinsbourne 1974). The Apposition of Opposites and other hypnotic language patterns help facilitate the balancing of these seemingly opponent psychological experiences without our having to make a conscious effort. This not only helps to install our new option of accepting both extremes and balancing between them, but mirrors, and thus can utilize, the natural response of the nervous system itself to continually recreate balance.

With the unconscious mind aware that both extremes are needed, complementary, and require each other to exist as they are, a certain experience of paradox begins to arise. Experientially, it feels as if a mental "gap" arises, or the circuits of the Direction Filter seem to overload and blow out. As we learn to harness the energy of that direction process to propel us *toward* the experience of Both/And, and *away* from the experience of Either/Or, those moments or "gaps" accelerate, giving us access to more and more experiences of bare attention, or awareness without judgement or reaction.

nd as the silent sound of that knowing . . .
falls gently arising from within . . .
allowing its heightened depths to speak forth . . .
the rough smoothness of the journey . . .
continuing to emerge . . .

allowing that opened closure . . .

to continue its contracting expansion . . .

as the moving stillness . . . reaches out inward . . .

towards even deeper heights of understanding . . .

without judgement . . .

without comparison . . .

you can rest at ease now . . .

and relax . . .

With Facticity, the work done in altered states of consciousness makes liberal use of many hypnotic language patterns. Students of Ericksonian Hypnosis will recognize these as TDS, phonological and punctuation ambiguities, covering all possible classes of response, and embedded and interspersed suggestion, all fostering the process of indirect associative focusing (see Glossary). Skillfully used language patterns can uproot previous language associations and allow a fluid reassociation to occur in the manner desired.

Chapter 15

The Mind and How it Creates the Experience of Duality

". . . Pleasure and rage, sadness and joy, hopes and regrets,
change and stability, weakness and decision, impatience and
sloth: all are sounds from the same flute, all mushrooms from
the same wet mould. Day and night follow one another and
come upon us without our seeing how they sprout . . ."

The Way of Chuang Tzu
Thomas Merton

euro-Linguistic Programming and Ericksonian Hypnosis have given us many new tools and understandings about the mind and how it works to create
our subjective experience. Some of the most interesting insights arise when we apply this knowledge to explore how the
mind creates the experience of duality.

The major mental mechanisms creating subjective experience
(sub-modalities, sorting patterns, meta-programs — see Glossary) all have one particular *structure* and one particular *pattern*
in common. The structure is a range of possibility from one
extreme form of response to its opposite. The pattern is one of
movement from one extreme form to its opposite.

Some examples are:

Toward	Away
Positive	Negative
Match	Mismatch
Self	Other
External	Internal
Color	Black & White
Loud	Soft
Hot	Cold
Sweet	Sour
Fragrant	Acrid
Movement	Stillness
Light	Dark

For the seeker of mental health and spiritual insight, it is revolutionary to realize this is the *hardware* of the mind. The nature of the mechanisms of mind reflect the very presence of Opposites.

These mental mechanisms cannot be removed or destroyed, but they can be harnessed and used to propel us in a new direction.

A nd as the unconscious mind . . .

free now to continue those learnings . . .

expand that recognition . . .

hidden harmonies emerging . . .

continuing to sort through that vast realm of experience . . .

that is your experience . . .

unnoticed before . . .

yet now available in a new light . . .

grasped in a new way . . .

free to voice its words of wisdom held silent before . . .

allowing that awareness to arise . . .

of how those two things so seemingly opposed . . .

dance together . . .

in the deep rhythm of now . . .

and how creative can that unconscious mind be . . .

shifting those perceptions now . . .

towards that direction of accepting . . .

relaxing . . .

and allowing what is . . .

to be . . .

can't you ? . . .

The entire mind/body system operates on recognition which requires comparison. From major mental judgements and discriminations down to the very cells of the forming embryo that somehow "know" how to recognize and move to the correct tissue or organ, *comparison is a basic strategy of mind and body.*

Regulation systems of the body also use forms of matching and mis-matching (sorting for similarities and sorting for differences) to recognize states of balance and imbalance, i.e. homeostasis. As long as comparison is the basic way in which the mind/body functions, differences are required — and those differences exist on a continuum that spans from one extreme form to its opposite. Without them, recognition cannot occur.

When seekers of mental health or spiritual awareness reach the understanding that judgement and comparison is, in fact, what causes the majority of mental and emotional problems, they are left in a dilemma. Where to go for that non-judgemental awareness? Where to go for the choiceless awareness? Where to go for that proverbial peace that passes all understanding?

As our understanding of how the mind works become clearer and clearer, it is obvious there is no way we can understand oneness *through the mind* without relaxing into oneness as the organic unity of the two.

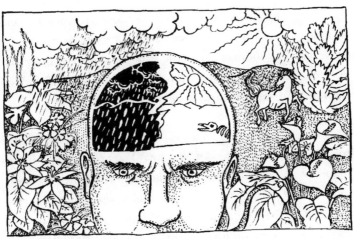

conflict is in the mind

The more we can recognize the nature and structure of mental functions and allow them to be what they are, the more creative we can become in using those mechanisms to propel us, in a healthy and safe way, toward mental health and spiritual insight.

The Facticity process recognizes mental health as living out of a relaxed mind involved in the joys of creatively living. Yet, how is it possible for the mind to relax when its very structure of operation is comparing and choosing? The very mechanisms of mind are designed to direct our energies either toward a desirable outcome or away from an undesirable outcome.

This basic, undeniable and unalterable experience of duality is created by and intrinsic to the mind itself. The mental mechanism of comparison is basic to all sensory experience and thus, the mind's representation of that experience — linguistically and sensorially. For example, in order for the brain to register sound, it must also know silence. In order to register a sound as loud, it must also know soft. Most of us have no way to move beyond comparison as the way in which we make our choices. In addition, our current choices are primarily based upon the Aristotelian view of Either/Or.

When we have created a life rich with choices and excellence (major desired outcomes of NLP work), *and* reached a recognition of the Facticity of Opposites, choicelessness or non-judgemental awareness as a psychological option may become the next desired outcome. A mind that understands how its own perceptions are formed, and recognizes the intelligence and validity of moving to higher perceptions that transcend itself, will then use its intelligence, creativity and sensitivity to support that movement toward the beyond.

nd sometimes a person can . . .

become like a tree . . .

cut off from its roots . . .

and it's quite possible that a tree . . .

cut off from its roots might consider fragrance . . .

a mere fantasy . . .

a tree cut off from its roots . . .

might consider flowers . . .

an illusion to be dispelled . . .

a tree cut off from its roots . . .

might feel no meaning in its existence there, yet . . .

a tree cut off from its roots . . .

is no longer connected with life itself . . .

and as that tree might watch another . . .

whose roots are deeply embraced by the earth . . .

filling itself . . .

with the very stuff of which life is made . . .

why that tree might watch another blossoming its flowers . . .

and might even smell the fragrance . . .

but without its roots . . .

that tree will never have its own flowers opening . . .

its own fruit ripe and sweet with juice . . .

readying itself to burst forth and flow . . .

yet life, hungry to live . . .

finds its way even when the roots are cut . . .

to a new place where new roots can take root again . . .

and even the grass knows how . . .

to find its way through the hardness of the concrete street . . .

to continue its reach for the sky . . .

The mind is not the enemy. It is an incredible source of clarity and organization and creative expression. And it does work in *directions* (for and against, toward and away). If we want to create balance as a real choice, we must harness that directional power of the mind and use it. Through Facticity, we are exploring just this to help us reach that place where we can step out of mind and its perceptions of duality into the loving arms of our inner nature just awaiting our arrival home.

Notes:

Chapter 16

Fundamental Facticities

*". . . Sea water is at once very pure and very foul. It is drinkable
and healthful for fishes, but undrinkable and deadly for men.
The nature of day and night is one. The way up and the way
down are one and the same. Even sleepers are workers and
collaborators in what goes on in the universe. In the circle the
beginning and the end are common . . ."*

Heraclitus
Greek Mystic

A s we can recognize by now, the most fundamental
pattern in the fabric of life does appear to be the
Facticity of Opposites. The following is a list, incomplete of course, of many Opposites pinpointed and worked
with by many going through the Facticity Experience (a group
process).

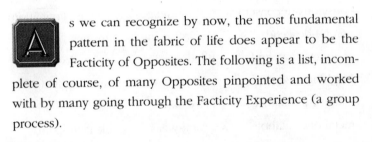

summer-winter	spring-fall	day-night
hot-cold	high-low	mountain-valley
movement-stillness	male-female	high tide-low tide
pond-stream	noisy-quiet	birth-death
clear-hazy	white-black	dark-light
wild-tame	sweet-sour	hard-soft
near-far	hungry-full	full-empty
smooth-rough	positive-negative	superficial-deep
seed-flower	ocean-raindrop	ocean-shore

ice-water · blooming-wilting · hiding-seeking

sow-reap · land-sea · earth-sky

gravity-levitation · fire-water · silence-sound

in-out · up-down · sickness-health

fresh-rotten · fertile-barren · fast-slow

sharp-blunt · awake-asleep · young-old

beginning-end · front-back · eating-being eaten

attack-retreat · protect-expose · misery-happiness

attraction-repulsion · action-reaction · passive-active

center-circumference · sunrise-sunset · giving-receiving

distant-close · light-heavy · floating-sinking

coming-going · rising-falling · height-depth

right-left · top-bottom · inside-outside

conscious-unconscious · tension-relaxation · intake-elimination

ascend-descend · stuck-flowing · arteries-veins

contracted-expanded · blind-seeing · open-closed

laughing-weeping · tall-short · standing-lying

balance-imbalance · hairy-bald · fat-thin

metabolic-catabolic · strong-weak · pleasure-pain

voluntary-involuntary · inhale-exhale · acid-alkaline

extension-flexion · old-young · body-soul

stiff-flexible · big-small · curly-straight

loud-soft · present-absent · right-wrong

anger-compassion · alone-together · agony-ecstasy

security-insecurity · spicy-bland · solid-liquid

acceptance-rejection · trust-doubt · love-hate

change-permanence · useful-useless · madness-sanity

energized-lethargic · fresh-stale · clarity-confusion

knowledge-ignorance · wet-dry · true-false

At the psychological level, it appears that most problems are rooted in the way we relate to one or more of the following four sets of Opposites.

Security/Insecurity: This manifests in many ways for different people. For some, it is hidden in approval-disapproval, acceptance-rejection, aloneness-togetherness. For others, it is wealth-poverty, recognition-anonymity, tasteful-tacky. Whatever language used in the individual map, the basic quest is for a permanent state of "no change". Once the unconscious mind grasps and sees and hears the rhythm of inevitable and constant change, it begins to become clear that ultimate security might reside in the acceptance of insecurity as the nature of life itself.

nd even as you rest here now . . .

the need to move . . .

to be still . . .

the need to focus . . .

the need to drift . . .

the changes come and go . . .

and your unconscious mind can become aware . . .

of its ability to relax with change . . .

to know now . . .

change is as natural as that breath . . .

bringing in fresh oxygen . . .

in exchange for that carbon dioxide . . .

going out with each exhalation . . .

and isn't it curious to become aware . . .

of change that is natural . . .

to being alive . . .

to being a part of existence . . .

that stretches and creates itself anew with each breath . . .

Life/Death: Most of us know that death will come to us at some time. And it appears the unconscious mind has specific ideas on how to respond to that. The unconscious mind is basically against death and for life — which is, of course, an intelligent choice. Biologically, it is the only choice. Psychologically, however, we can expand our unconscious understanding of death from a phenomena that brings with it the end of the body and the end of "me" toward a perception that death is *both* the completion of one phase *and* the beginning of another. Nature demonstrates this phenomena endlessly and allows us to recognize that endings and beginnings, life and death, are a natural circle of completion that allows the process of life to go on recreating itself fresh and new.

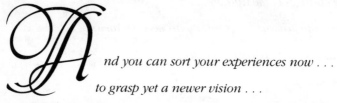

nd you can sort your experiences now . . .

to grasp yet a newer vision . . .

tuning in to the harmony . . .

hidden in that changing of forms . . .

occurring throughout life . . .

for with every death . . .

does come a birth . . .

and like that body . . .

dying to its form as a baby . . .

taking birth as that toddler's body . . .

so wobbly and brave . . .

moving on to yet another loss . . .

of that baby tooth . . .

which every child knows . . .

signifies the beginning of the end of being that child . . .

readying itself then to step forth . . .

and create the space for that adult tooth . . .

and long before the rest of the body . . .

becomes that adult body fully . . .

something deep inside that child knows . . .

it's time to begin the end . . .

and allow the new beginning to begin . . .

just as something deep . . .

within a seed planted in the earth . . .

knows . . .

there will come a time . . .

when its casing must crack . . .

and it will die to being that seed . . .

freeing itself . . .

to take the shape of a seedling . . .

free now . . .

to continue on . . .

the next stage of that journey . . .

continually emerging . . .

isn't it? . . .

Pleasure/Pain: Again, it is biological intelligence to move toward pleasure and to move away from pain. Psychological intelligence, however, calls us to alert the unconscious mind to the *value* of pain or unpleasant experiences whether physical, emotional or mental. In helping create value for the usually avoided experiences of pressure and pain, we can begin to relax our avoidance of these undeniable experiences of living and explore approaching them with new attitudes of response, i.e., learning, curiosity, relaxation, meditation.

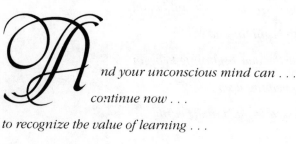

nd your unconscious mind can . . .

continue now . . .

to recognize the value of learning . . .

how to use that pain . . .

those endings . . .

that pressure . . .

just like the birds know how to use the pressure of the air . . .

to soar among the clouds . . .

and even the fish in the sea . . .

use the pressure of the deep waters . . .

to help them swim . . .

to be free to move and explore . . .

the deepest realms of the rich depths there below . . .

why even the littlest clams . . .

that make their way . . .

know how to use pressure . . .

moving themselves to travel where they want to go . . .

and even your own body knows . . .

how to use that experience of pressure . . .

to help you walk . . .

to lift up a foot and allow the pressure to shift . . .

naturally . . .

easily . . .

onto that other foot . . .

carrying you forward . . .

Alone/Together: The dilemma of the human heart is our need to be connected with each other, and our need to be unique, special and/or alone. This is one of our most basic inside-splits. Most of us are solidly identified with either alone-ness or togetherness as the "right" way to be, or the way to happiness. Those of us who have chosen togetherness, usually don't *experientially* know our own uniqueness and full presence when alone. Those of us who have chosen aloneness usually don't *experientially* know the validity of connectedness as a human need and a human condition. Through Facticity, we are working to validate both needs as equal, natural and complementary.

A *nd at the very bottom of the sea . . .*

lies the depth . . .

of the highest mountain peak . . .

for even the highest peak . . .

remains connected to the deepest depth of the earth . . .

the islands as they peek above the surface of the waters . . .

rising unique and alone in their expression . . .

can trust that knowing far below the surface of the sea . . .

they remain a part of the wholeness of the earth . . .

and the depths rest peacefully . . .

trusting their connection to that which is high above . . .

reaching toward those stars . . .

those skies where the birds can fly free . . .

and everyone has seen a bird soar in the sky . . .

and some might think the bird feels unconnected . . .

disconnected . . . alone . . .

yet birds that fly together in that flock . . .

connect with each other in a mysterious way . . .

yet each free in the only way you can . . .

fly on your own is alone . . .

and yet, together . . .

the birds connect in a form . . .

and fly through the skies together connected . . .

through a form and shape that remains . . .

a mystery to the mind . . .

and yet . . .

the birds can feel the connection, the pull, the direction . . .

that guides them . . .

on their way to reach that destination now . . .

relaxing with that journey . . .

traveling . . .

alone together . . .

For a thorough demonstration of the use of hypnotic language patterns in evoking and creating the search for these new points of view, see *Lions In Wait*. The first five chapters deal with these fundamental facticities.

Chapter 17

New Alternatives of Response — Relaxing into the Flow

". . . Do not divide. Roots and flowers are two ends of one phenomenon . . ."

Om Mani Padma Hum
Osho

ur current unconscious response to Opposites is to choose. In order to reach the new option of choicelessness, certain guidelines may need to be established. The following are five major sets of Opposites *as perceived through the mind* that can offer alternatives of response, and hopefully answer general objections and concerns to new points of view.

Balance/Imbalance: With Facticity, we are exploring the continual re-creation of balance as a major strategy for relaxing with duality. The unconscious mind generally takes the verb "to balance" and makes it into a noun, some "place" to reach and stay. We can expand the unconscious mind's understanding of balance to a process constantly recreating itself, i.e. balancing in motion. Imbalance then is simply a part of the balancing process, and the experience through which balance arises.

nd that balancing is a state of motion . . .

just as you learned when walking . . .

to allow the body its movement . . .

to re-establish that balance . . .

from moment to moment as you moved . . .

almost like walking on a tightrope . . .

knowing if the movement is too far toward one side . . .

a fall will be coming . . .

a movement too far to the other side, a fall will be coming . . .

and the landing is seemingly always on another tightrope . . .

where the balancing begins again . . .

and just as the body allows the balancing to come . . .

when it stands ever so still . . .

yet continuing to sway . . .

in its own way . . .

back and forth . . .

side to side . . .

continually recreating balance . . .

allowing the natural flow . . .

from one side to the other side to be the natural flow . . .

as the balancing allows the natural . . .

balance . . .

to reach . . .

that state of constant motion . . .

where imbalance becomes balance . . .

again and again . . .

as easy as breathing in . . .

and breathing out . . .

Trust/Doubt: We generally find little value in the experience of doubt. However, doubt can be powerful feedback that keeps us searching for the experiences we seek of undeniable knowing. For most of us, true trust has almost been lost. The trust we usually speak of refers to "hoping I'll get what I want". With Facticity, we are exploring that the kind of trust more valuable to us may be more akin to following an inner pull or knowing that takes us into the unknown, without guarantees of any kind.

A nd there are rhythms of movement . . .

that have nothing to do . . .

with the external world of light and dark . . .

of warmth and cold . . .

even a tiny bean seedling . . .

lifting its leaves at daybreak stretching towards the sun . . .

lowering those leaves at night when it falls . . .

the bean seedling continues this movement . . .

even in constant darkness . . .

following its intrinsic, intuitive rhythm . . .

of movement and change . . .

and some plants . . .

allow that mysterious process of photosynthesis . . .

changing that light into energy . . .

comes to its peak in the midday . . .

and drops to a low at night . . .

and even when there is no light . . .

the plant uses its learnings . . .

of how to transform and create energy . . .

and many seeds even in an unchanging place . . .

will germinate and grow faster in the spring and summer . . .

regardless of what's really going on around them . . .

and its curious to realize . . .

these intrinsic rhythms flow . . .

in their own rhythm . . .

allowing a process to occur . . .

that is a natural process now . . .

Usefulness/Uselessness: Most of us generally feel bad about being useless. So once again we can explore its value and necessity to the expression of being useful. Pinpointing experiences that are useful at one time and useless at other times help the unconscious mind begin to relax. For example, a closed fist is very useful for writing, holding a fork, and carrying a brief case. However, a hand that can never open and relax will eventually cramp and become useless in a negative way. A positive uselessness would be the open hand, fingers stretched and palm empty, allowing the hand to rest. And this uselessness becomes useful for receiving many things a closed hand could never grasp. The purpose here is to create a basically positive mind without denying or ignoring the darker or unpleasant realities of experiential living. It is known to be much easier to step into Mental Health and No-Mind from gratitude (a positive state) than from grief (a negative state).

J ust as the unconscious mind . . .

can continue now . . .

learning to whisper its hidden wisdoms aloud . . .

like the waters of the brook . . .

distinctive in its babbling that goes on and on . . .

can only be heard . . .

because of the rocks in that brook . . .

although for another those rocks might only be rocks . . .

to the brook, it allows its song to be sung . . .

and for a person with an eye that can see . . .

why the rocks in the brook can become stepping stones . . .

used to help a person cross from one place to another . . .

and the stones upon which a person steps . . .

can be different stones for different people . . .

for a stepping stone . . .

that's used to help a person cross . . .

is chosen by the walker alone . . .

as they progress along the distance . . .

towards where they want to go . . .

leaving what has been of service and is no more . . .

behind them now where it belongs . . .

free to assist another . . .

and allow that usefulness to arise again . . .

Consciousness/Unconsciousness: Most spiritual seekers perceive consciousness, enlightenment, awareness, or anything of the spiritual nature, as something to be attained, earned, or achieved. Through Facticity, we are exploring whether what we are in search of is actually already here and already ours. Acceptance and relaxation allow us to fall back inside what is naturally ours to know, i.e. our spiritual nature. There is also great relief and value in recognizing unconsciousness as necessary and intrinsic to the expansion of conscious awareness itself.

*Y*our unconscious mind continuing now . . .

   to explore that possibility . . .

   awareness is yours . . .

to use . . . to step into . . .

anytime you remember now . . .

for life itself all around you lives . . .

in the very atmosphere itself . . .

that nearly transparent envelope . . .

of gases and particles, surrounding the earth . . .

the atmosphere playing a crucial role . . .

in the very existence of life . . .

for that atmosphere exists all around . . .

enveloping with its transparency . . .

yet transporting water . . .

from the oceans to the land itself . . .

transmitting radiation from the sun . . .

so essential to those green plants being free . . .

to turn that light . . .

into energy . . .

the atmosphere shielding the earth . . .

from those lethal ultra-violet rays and meteor showers . . .

acting as a blanket . . .

covering the earth . . .

maintaining its temperature . . .

cooling the torrid heat of the tropics . . .

warming the barren coldness of the polar caps . . .

and that atmosphere moves and carries sound . . .

and electromagnetic waves . . .

allowing communication to occur . . .

and that atmosphere . . . surrounding . . .

an essential key . . .

to the unlocking of life . . . itself . . .

and somewhere in that atmosphere rests . . . the sky . . .

and can the sky be somewhere when its everywhere? . . .

can the sky be somewhere . . . specific . . .

when the sky is always here? . . .

Self/No-Self: Mystical maps often refer to ultimate reality as Oneness, No-Thingness, Suchness and other interesting and often confusing labels. Whatever the label, there is sure to follow the concept of surrender, or losing one's self. This idea can paralyze, numb, and completely divert the mind from going on with the seeker's exploration — both consciously and unconsciously. Any proposition of death, even that of an "ego death" can be viewed by the unconscious mind as dangerous. With Facticity, we are exploring an alternative perception of "self" or "ego" so the unconscious mind can relax with the possibility of discovering that we are in fact a part of the whole, and that the whole is even greater than the sum of its parts.

nd your unconscious mind . . .

can explore now . . .

just how it is that a person can . . .

draw many lines on a piece of paper that was blank . . .

criss-crossing those lines like lines of energy . . .

and where many lines cross a point . . .

a point begins to arise . . .

that wasn't there before . . .

a point that appears solid to the eye . . .

separate from the lines . . .

crossing back and forth across the page . . .

and when many lines cross back and forth . . .

why a big point arises . . .

a dot . . .

right there . . .

and is a point really there . . .

separate from those lines . . .

or is it a part of the motion and the movement all around . . .

the coming to a comfortable place . . .

where the point seems to be ?. . .

For complete trance-scripts demonstrating movement toward these alternative responses, see *Lions In Wait.*

Chapter 18

Identity — Stepping Stone to the Beyond

". . . Destroy the ego? Hound it, beat it, snub it, tell it where it gets off? Great fun, no doubt. But, where is it? Must you not find it first? Isn't there a word about catching your goose before you cook it? The great difficulty here is that there isn't one . . ."

Parable of The Goose
Wei Wu Wei

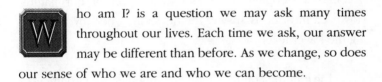ho am I? is a question we may ask many times throughout our lives. Each time we ask, our answer may be different than before. As we change, so does our sense of who we are and who we can become.

Up to now we've been exploring how to utilize our discounted experience to enhance mental health — particularly, those discounted experiences indicating life really is a process going on and on and on, changing from one moment to the next, in ordered and creative patterns. Meditation explores the application of these same discounted experiences to the concepts of "self" and "I" or identity.

From a psychological perspective, there appears to be different levels of change that can impact our behavior. Logically, changes in the higher levels will automatically cause shifts in the lower levels, while change in the lower levels may not necessarily effect higher level functioning. These levels from highest to lowest are:

Spiritual	
Identity	(who)
Beliefs and Values	(why)
Capabilities	(how)
Behaviors	(what)
Environment	(when/where)

If we are interested in exploring the spiritual level, identity becomes a stepping stone into that aspect of our nature. However, most of us answer the question "who?" by referencing the lower levels.

I live in the South. = *I am* a Southerner. (environment)

I told the truth. = *I am* an honest person. (behavior)

I write books. = *I am* a writer. (capability)

It is important to be smart. = *I am* stupid. (belief/value)

Following the understanding that a problem can't be solved with the same level of thinking that created it, it seems clear that issues of identity can more usefully be explored from higher level perceptions, rather than lower. Recognition of "who?" from insights at the spiritual level bring a dramatically powerful reorganization and reassociation of experience, i.e., the conversion experience, satori, awakening, enlightenment.

At this level, the exploration of self/no-self is a natural step following all the others, and usually unfolds as our inner environment becomes ripe to receive it.

The idea of "me" presupposes "you" and a separation. The unconscious mind assumes this separation to be true and begins to solidify the *process* of our life journey into a thing — into something concrete. "*This* is who I am!" "I" is a useful and necessary concept, needed to work in the world, to communicate in the world, and to move in the world. And, there are times when that solid sense of "me" as a separate, non-changing personality, gets in the way of getting along, of moving easily, and of being able to learn and to flow.

Each of us who wants to live as a healthy human being, in the world, capable of functioning and producing, must develop a minimum of two basic skills relating to our sense of self. The first is the ability to stand up for ourself. If we don't have a solid sense of "me" as an individual with our own needs and desires, we will generally let others walk all over us. The second is the ability to step aside. If we can't put our "ego" away and step to the side, it becomes very difficult to learn, and often, to simply get along.

Western psychology basically deals with discovering the self and the ability to stand up for the self. Eastern psychology basically deals with putting the self aside and discovering a higher level beyond self. As Westerners, most of our stepping aside is done out of compromise and a belief that it is necessary to survival. It is expanding to have the choice of stepping aside because we want to, recognizing the benefit and beauty of "nobody being home" as well as the benefit and beauty of "being there".

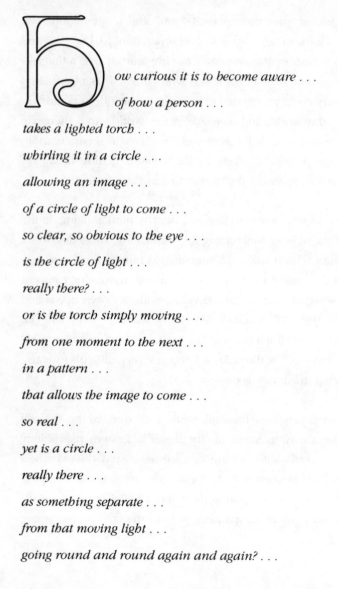

ow curious it is to become aware . . .

of how a person . . .

takes a lighted torch . . .

whirling it in a circle . . .

allowing an image . . .

of a circle of light to come . . .

so clear, so obvious to the eye . . .

is the circle of light . . .

really there? . . .

or is the torch simply moving . . .

from one moment to the next . . .

in a pattern . . .

that allows the image to come . . .

so real . . .

yet is a circle . . .

really there . . .

as something separate . . .

from that moving light . . .

going round and round again and again? . . .

Can a sense of no-self, or putting ourself aside, really be useful in the world? In the Taoist writings of Chuang Tzu, there is a story of an empty boat. Just imagine yourself out in a boat, laying down in its bottom and floating across the water, feeling the sun, enjoying the gentle movements, when you feel a crash, and you know you've run into something. You sit up and look out and there is another boat, and there's somebody in it. You find yourself irritated because you were lying there in the sun, having a nice time, day dreaming and this idiot isn't looking where he's going and knocks into your boat and disrupts your fantasies. So, you find yourself angry and saying, "Why don't you look where you're going, fella? Wake Up!!" So he goes on his way and you lay back down in your boat, get all stretched out again, comfortable and relaxed, just laying there, floating along, and it happens again — another crash! So, you quickly sit up, ready to lash out. And you see there is another boat there, but this time, there's nobody in it — just a boat floating around, empty. So you just reach out, push it away, and lay back down in your boat and go on.

If we can be an empty boat when we need to be, we can move through life with much less difficulty. There are times in life when we'd like to be like an empty boat and can't be. The sense of "me" is sometimes so strong we have no choice but to defend it, even if we don't want to. The desire to be right can be so strong we find ourselves ready to fight to the end for our rightness. And there are times when we don't really care whether we're right or not. We just want to do what we're doing and can't because that sense of self, of who we are, is so strong we can't let go.

the empty boat

Most of us have had times when we needed to stick up for ourself and defend ourself, because it was important and nourishing to our sense of self-worth. And many times, we were unable to recognize and solidify our uniqueness, individuality and worth so that we could do so.

There have been times when we may have wished we didn't have to stick so strongly to who we thought we were, or what our principles were, or beliefs or ideas, because it was just not worth it. And we found ourselves unable to step outside that defending posture and just relax and allow.

To live in true mental health is to have both options — holding our ground, *and* putting our self aside when appropriate, practical and safe to do so. In keeping with the Facticity of Opposites, when *mind* creates the reality of self, there must also be its opposite of no-self.

If we don't experientially know the value of both self and no-self at the psychological level, it is often too big a jump for the psyche into the spiritual realm of no-self and oneness. **And it is important to recognize these are learnings and knowings from *different* levels of our nature.** If the hologram model of the spiritual realm is accurate, it is psychologically too much to ask a part to dissolve into the whole without first knowing that it is truly a part of that whole, unique in itself, and that dissolution will be an expansion and a fullness rather than a death and an emptiness (in the negative sense of the word).

the clinging dewdrop

This sense of ourselves as separate is actually a *psychological* truth. It is something that is accurate psychologically for every single one of us. Nobody's going to say there is not somebody here. We're all here in the sense that we are all individuals, each with our own name, our own experience, our own private worlds, private minds and private lives. Most of us will also agree there are times when it is appropriate, practical and safe to put our sense of self aside. The learning process itself requires this action.

However, from that point of view *outside the mind*, a different level "truth" is reported and then expressed in a variety of ways — no-self, oneness, cosmic consciousness, connectedness, emptiness.

A dilemma for many spiritual seekers is the "ego" has not yet been psychologically solidified and there is not yet a strong sense of self to set aside. Consequently, efforts to live "selflessly" from spiritual insights are often followed by confusion and even despair arising from the unfulfilled psychological level.

One well traveled avenue towards oneness often includes denying or ignoring our psychological need for a solid sense of self (identity). With Facticity, we are exploring if there is another way to move towards behavior that demonstrates these insights from our spiritual nature, and allow true mental health as well?

During medieval times, the whole world believed the sun revolved around the earth and that the earth was flat. There was no-one who didn't believe that. Yet, sailors who frequently roamed the seas would be heard to say the world was round and there were very strange things on the other side.

The sailors figured the earth was round because when they were out on the ocean they could see the ships coming from afar. They would see the tops of the ships first — the high masts — and then the whole ship would come into view, top to bottom. This perspective made them think the earth must be round.

Then the astronomers began to say the sailors were right. The earth was round, and what's more, it actually revolved around the sun.

Now for the people of that time, it was absolutely mind-boggling to imagine the earth they were standing on so calmly to be actually turning completely around every single day. They couldn't see the earth moving, or feel the movement as it turned. They couldn't imagine that the sun, which they could see moving across the sky with their own eyes, was actually remaining in one spot with the earth moving around *it*. But the astronomers were saying this was the way it was.

Those people had a tremendous challenge put forth to them because psychologically the sun does appear to move around the earth, and we still experience it that way today. The sun rises and it sets and that's a psychological reality for every one of us. Psychologically, the earth does appear to be flat, and we still experience it that way now.

Yet, scientifically, that is not the way it is. The earth actually is round and does move around the sun. The sun stays still in relation to us, and we move around it. It must have been a rather difficult experience to be told the way they were perceiving was inaccurate from another point of view, because psychologically and sensorially, their conclusions were totally logical and experientially true.

When we move into working with the idea of no-self, it is a similar situation. There is some part of each of us that goes — what? — this is absurd! And to the logical mind, it is. Yet, when we choose from our own experience and knowledge that we don't want to fight, we just want to let things be the way they are and be happy inside, there must be some way to step out of the idea there is somebody here that we have to fight for and defend.

The medieval analogy points out that a leap of trust is necessary to move beyond our psychological perceptions to perceptions of another level. Now not everyone went off to find out for themselves that the earth was round, but many sailors did — many adventurers.

And Facticity is for adventurers — people who aren't satisfied with simply believing. People who want to experientially "know" higher level perception for themselves. Adventurers have always had that quality of trust, or willingness, to go into the unknown and discover for themselves what was there. The medieval people had a great challenge — to accept something that made all their beliefs up to that time seem inaccurate. Some were even killed for holding these "new" beliefs, burned at the stake and forced to recant.

There is a story that the head of the church brought Galileo before him and demanded that he remove from his treatises the paragraphs where he stated the earth was moving around the sun. Galileo is said to have replied, with a great sense of humor, "No problem, I can remove this assertion from my writings . . . but remember, the earth will still go on moving around the sun, regardless of what I say. It will not take any notice of me. The earth does not read my books."

the earth is not flat

Unless we understand these different levels of the mind and beyond, it is extremely difficult to let go of a belief rooted in a psychological truth and consider perceptions from another aspect of our nature.

Now we might assume that we can't know for ourselves that the earth is round and that it's moving. But astronauts know the earth is round — experientially — and they know the earth is moving — through their own experience. Most of us are either ill-equipped or unwilling to take the risks necessary to gather that experiential knowing for ourselves. However, if we have the capacities and the willingness, Facticity offers some tips on how to travel this mental and spiritual terrain with a bit more ease for the mind.

To expand ourselves beyond the level of our minds into a true experience of our body and spirit or whatever other dimensions we might be, we have to be willing to step outside of our psychological truths — honoring them for what they are — yet free to explore truths from other levels of our nature that are beyond psychology (mind).

If we are in fact body, mind and spirit, then we must explore expanding ourselves to a vast enough perspective to include all our dimensions and whatever seeming contradictions arise. Ultimately, the mind/body reality in which we live *is* a paradox simply because its very nature is dual. It is only when Opposites are in absolute balance that they cancel each other out, leaving neither one nor the other with any more push or pull.

Entry into the dimension holding the spiritual insights we seek is more easily allowed as that balancing of seeming Opposites continues to occur, essentially cancelling themselves out — and creating space for whole new perceptions to arise.

Self is a psychological truth rooted in the experience of our uniqueness. No-self is a truth of a different nature, yet rooted in direct experience of our connectedness. Perhaps our connectedness is akin to the reality of the earth moving around the sun and being round. It is possible to acquire that reality experientially and thus begin to know there really isn't anybody home, *and* there is — leaving the mind with a balancing to come into being. That balancing creates the centerpoint that can catapult us toward new dimensions of experience beyond the mind.

recognition of opposites as complimentary can create a "gap" in the mind

A person who is balancing in the psychological realities of self and no-self can more easily continue on to seek their identity at the spiritual level as well.

167

Notice the first drawing of the plant below. At first, all you will
see are the leaves and the pot. Now, look at the space between
the leaves. It's a different way of perceiving the picture, is it
not? And you end up seeing different things. Unless you're an
artist, aware of how to utilize "negative space", you've probably been trained, both consciously and unconsciously, not to
notice the space and to focus only on the leaves — even
though the experience of the space is there to experience.

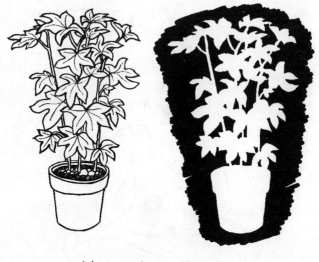

positive and negative space

By using this approach, it is the *space* that then defines the
presence of the leaves. If you draw the leaves by drawing the
space only and not the lines of the leaves themselves, you'll
end up with the same picture, but will have traveled a completely different route, with a completely different experience,
i.e., something arising out of nothing.

By alerting the mind that 1) space is there to experience, and 2) it is alright to look at it from this point of view, all the space between the leaves that was unnoticed before comes into view. Awareness of no-self can arise in a similar fashion. By shifting our approach, that which *defines* or creates our sense of self begins to come to the foreground.

Joseph Goldstein once posed this interesting question — "Is there really a Big Dipper?". I had to ponder that. The Big Dipper was certainly there in my perception, but it was only there by my mind's action of connecting those stars with imaginary lines existing *only* in my mind. So, the Big Dipper both exists and doesn't exist.

In some sumi art, lines in various shapes and angles and relationships are drawn without connecting them together to give a complete and concrete image. This process evokes the unconscious mind's ability to take those basically meaningless and disconnected scribbles and make them into something meaningful — a face, a tree, an animal, a house, a flower.

the mind completes the drawing

At the psychological level, the mental mechanisms involved in creating and perpetuating the sense of ourselves as some "one" separate and solid are the same mechanisms evoked and utilized in sumi art. This is a physiological parallel to the creation of nominalizations and TDS phenomena (see Glossary) in linguistics which add to the psychological reality of the sense of "I".

Content-free meditation can reveal this same process occurring in the creation of "I" as a concrete thing — real and separate and unchanging. The mind's need to create meaning (see TDS Phenomena in Glossary) of whatever arises in its field of experience forces this search for meaning. Even those perceptions and experiences that arise from beyond the mind are funneled through the same meaning-making process, thus creating some mental representation that seems solid and real.

When we dis-identify with the mind (and its emotions) as *who* we are, these processes can more clearly be experienced and verified moment to moment.

And it is important to remember that healthy dis-identification from the mind frees us to fully associate with our sensory experiences of the present.

My own experience of the creative flow that arises when I'm doing sessions or trainings is like a series of waves that arise and pass away from moment to moment. I have learned to ride those waves allowing their presence and their intensity, with an acute awareness that I have nothing to do with their creation or their presence. They are more of a "happening" than anything else.

riding on the wave of creativity

However, when the creative flow is finished for awhile, some part of me always wants to take credit for the creativity that arose. Yet I know, experientially, that creativity was not made to happen by me. And what's more, when I try to "make it happen", failure is certain to come. The creativity only arises when "I" am out of the way, creating an inner environment that seems to invite this phenomenon to flow and express itself in its own way.

It is a fascinating process to watch your own mind crystallize and solidify the flow of your own experience through these mental mechanisms into a sense of separate self or ego. As this continues becoming clearer, and grounding in sensory experience stronger, more moments of connecting with the spiritual sense of no-self or oneness naturally begin to occur. And with it, may come yet another new answer to the question "Who am I?" — or perhaps the disappearance of the questioner himself.

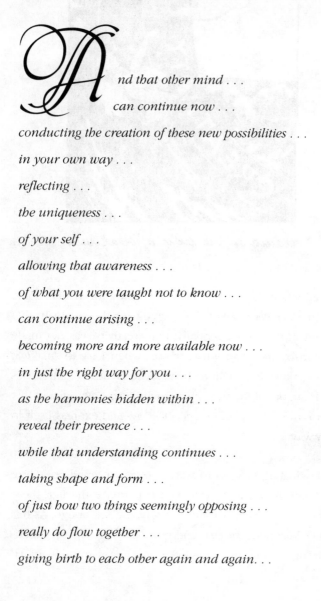

nd that other mind . . .

can continue now . . .

conducting the creation of these new possibilities . . .

in your own way . . .

reflecting . . .

the uniqueness . . .

of your self . . .

allowing that awareness . . .

of what you were taught not to know . . .

can continue arising . . .

becoming more and more available now . . .

in just the right way for you . . .

as the harmonies hidden within . . .

reveal their presence . . .

while that understanding continues . . .

taking shape and form . . .

of just how two things seemingly opposing . . .

really do flow together . . .

giving birth to each other again and again. . .

Notes:

Chapter 19

Facticity and NLP

". . . Do not search for the truth; only cease to cherish opinions . . ."
Sengsten
3rd Zen Patriarch

euro-Linguistic Programming proves to be a magnificent set of tools for working with subjective reality. And the NLP community continues uncovering new depths of understanding seemingly almost every day. However, as it stands now, the NLP model remains a closed system with no way out of the mind itself.

NLP places consciousness as a by-product of human experience; that is, its existence is contingent on the existence of the mind/body. It is defined as a by-product of the relative signal intensity of neural activity, or dependent on brain activity for its presence. Facticity questions this most basic assumption.

The basis of both Eastern and Western mysticism is the existence of consciousness *without* an object to experience. This reality to which the mystics point is a final recognition that we are not the body, or the mind, but something referred to as consciousness, turiya, the fourth, suchness, No-Mind, and many other names.

As a model for movement beyond the mind, Facticity embraces the availability of many levels of consciousness, at least one of which transcends the mind/body phenomena (or the requirement of subject-object, observer-observed, in order to exist).

Transpersonal Psychology explores many non-ordinary states of consciousness, and is continuing to recognize their potential for healing and transformation. The influx of NLP knowledge into this field will surely increase the speed with which research can continue.

To assume that consciousness does not end with biological death or begin with biological birth may seem radical. Yet, it has been the basic presupposition of all mysticism throughout the ages. With Facticity, we are simply bringing this into conscious awareness and supporting its exploration at the unconscious level. This exploration includes pinpointing and offering experiential verification of two of the major points to which mystics speak — the reality of Opposites (or duality) as a creation of the mind — and oneness, as the ultimate nature of our being, only becoming understandable when dis-identification from the mind/body dynamic occurs.

In keeping with Gregory Bateson's model for logical levels of change, the spiritual remains the highest level. Thus, work done at this level will trickle down and cause automatic reorganization and change at other levels below. However, it is important to recognize we cannot work with the spiritual level *directly*.

The tastes we do have from that aspect of our nature must go through the mind as soon as we attempt to share, communicate, or remember. We, of necessity, begin talking "about" something that has already been subjected to deletion, distortion, generalization (see Glossary), and the unique filters of our own personal maps. To date, it seems that only those people who are dis-identified with the mind/body in a positive sense (Enlightened or Awakened ones) have the highest rate of success in helping others access insights from their spiritual nature.

The history of mystics interacting with others reveals an array of seemingly bizarre and illogical behaviors, all of which could be viewed as the creation of "situations" to help move the seeker beyond the mind.

Facticity is, in fact, based on the modeling of language patterns, presentation patterns, and presupposition challenges in the discourses of various Eastern and Western Mystics, both living and dead, such as Sengsten, Heraclitus, Buddha, Chuang Tzu, Lao Tzu, Joseph Goldstein, Jack Kornfeld, Paul Reps, and Osho.

With the East and West coming together in many new ways, it is time to also explore how the knowledge of NLP and the knowings of meditation can come together. An impact at the Identity level can be made, creating an opening in the system, a door to the beyond, a way out of the mind. This exploration is what Facticity is all about.

Chapter 20

Facticity and Meditation

". . . So, when the shoe fits, the foot is forgotten. When the belt fits, the belly is forgotten. When the heart is right, "for" and "against" are forgotten . . ."

The Way of Chuang Tzu
Thomas Merton

acticity draws from mystical teachings and the personal explorations of many modern-day seekers, including my own inward journey that began some 20 years ago. The invaluable insights and understandings arising from the practice of meditation have much practical value for our modern man. **And even more so, meditation is the balance for working with the mind**.

In a culture that creates new technology with lightening speed, and a world whose traditional foundations continue crumbling daily, the need for a new and radical approach seems called for. Something useful can arise as these two bodies of NLP knowledge and meditation experience come together.

Meditation communities around the world are recognizing that meditation, by itself, is simply not creating full mental health as it was presupposed it would. Consequently, many of us engaged in meditation are coming back to psychology in order to clean up our minds from past conditionings, fears, and wounds still unhealed. However, there remains confusion as to why the insights and understandings from meditation experience have not automatically created new behaviors.

Facticity is rooted in this question and looks to the field of unconscious communication for its answers, both Ericksonian Hypnosis and NLP. As was stated in the beginning of this book, whether we want to make a simple behavioral change, like giving up coffee, or go for the transformational experience of living moment to moment with non-judgemental awareness, the *unconscious mind* must be convinced that is the appropriate choice or no new behavior will be allowed.

The unconscious mind is the mind in charge of behavior and without its permission, no change will occur.

With Facticity, we are bringing together these powerful fields of knowledge. With access to NLP's recognition and organization of the mental mechanisms operating in the creation of subjective experience and duality, those of us meditating will find our own understandings of the mind deepening, and our attitudes relaxing. NLP provides the meditation community powerful tools to create the needed psychological clean-up more quickly.

Meditation knows the value of choiceless awareness and can recognize the value of NLP in accelerating the availability of this state of consciousness. Facticity honors that the *fabric* of the mind must remain the same, but explores weaving in a new *pattern of response*. When experience comes into the mind and is naturally split in two by the mind itself, it can come in through a filter that now offers a choice of choicelessness — a choice based in experiential knowing that we are everything. There is nothing to be denied. There is nothing to be against. There is nothing to be for. There is just to be.

reflections

Meditation offers the world of NLP insights into the nature of our reality beyond mind, and a way to open the doors of the house before the air goes bad and the smell becomes stale. A model of the mind with no way out of the mind does not match the experience of inner space explorers. Content-free meditation, whether in a passive or active form, provides a category of experience beyond the capacities of the current NLP model to hold. Facticity offers the first step in this coming together of both.

Our world is sleepily destroying itself daily. An acceleration of consciousness and non-judgemental awareness is desperately needed. NLP has the tools to help train the mind in the service of the heart — and create the next choice of choiceless awareness. The genius and the tools are here to explore *how* to have easier access to our nature beyond the mind.

Nothing has effected me more deeply than personally discovering that realm beyond mind. I am amazed at the willingness of my mind to now use its creativity and power toward acceptance of myself right now . . . and now . . . and now. Never has my heart been so often filled with gratitude toward life, and the continuing inner expansion of space to receive it just as it is.

I have been working with my mind and the minds of others, both conscious and unconscious, for many years now, and it is still a vast mystery. Our recognition of the mystery and the magic still seems lacking — the childlike awe, the sense of wonder, the remembering that we are just on a journey from here to here, and all there is to do, on the inside, is simply be where we are and who we are, naturally, and allow the process to unfold.

Notes:

Chapter 21

Facticity's Impact on Traditional Therapy

". . . He who wants to have right without wrong, order without disorder, does not understand the principles of heaven and earth. He does not know how things hang together. Can a man cling only to heaven and know nothing of earth? They are correlative; to know one is to know the other. To refuse one is to refuse both. Can a man cling to the positive without the negative in contrast to which it is seen to be positive? If he claims to do so, he is a rogue or a madman . . ."

The Way of Chuang Tzu
Thomas Merton

he major difference in traditional therapy/counseling and NLP is the differing emphasis on form and structure versus content. NLP highly values working with the form and structure of our experience, while therapy highly values working with the content of our experience. Whichever direction the mind moves us toward, the consciousness of the practitioner remains a part of the process, and an important part.

The more "non-ordinary" the consciousness of the people-helper, the more likely it is for the client to be perceived as "acceptable right now", a person who really is OK regardless of their presenting behavior.

The current stereotypes for these two categories of practitioner are very polarized. The therapist is often characterized by NLP as basically inept, but with a lot of heart to bring to the healing process. The NLP practitioner is often characterized by the therapist as capable of making change, but in a manipulative manner, and without a real heart-felt connection for the other's pain. Facticity would like to see the best of both extremes come together.

Each of us has both capacities. With Facticity, we are working to heal any separation in the healer himself. An exquisite mind without a connection to the knowings of the heart can only lead us astray. A heart that does not have access to the understandings and workings of mind can never gain the strength and clarity to lead modern man anywhere but in circles. Together, they have the power to lead us toward the wisdom of our Being and the open secrets of our spiritual nature with greater strength and increasing ease.

The idea of using the mind to move beyond the mind will cause most meditators to cringe in horror. The idea of bringing the heart into the structure of subjectivity will cause many NLP students to grimace with pain.

However, many NLP practitioners report discovering a kind of dead-end. Everything *is* better, but it's still not enough. And meditators know meditation does work, but seems to take forever and doesn't solve all the psychological problems.

Therapists and Practitioners must continue becoming the first adventurers. Our time is too short for anything but a coming together, a pooling of all our strengths and resources, and a trusting that we can create another way. Neither the heart nor the mind alone will transform our world or ourselves. We need both, and together, hand in hand, a bridge to beyond the mind can be created.

If you're interested in exploring yet another way, you're invited to join this dance of discovering the complementariness of both — the scientific and the spiritual, the heart and the mind, the earth and the sky, the visible and the invisible.

earth and sky dancing together

Appendix A

The Facticity Model's Basic Assumptions

". . . You cannot stay on the summit forever. You have to come down again, so why bother in the first place? Just this. What is above knows what is below, but what is below does not know what is above. One climbs and one sees; one descends and one sees no longer, but one has seen. There is an art of conducting oneself in the lower region by the memory of what one saw higher up. When one no longer sees, one can at least still know . . ."

Mount Analogue
Rene Daumal

1. Consciousness exists beyond the mind/body phenomena, without an object, and without the need for object-subject or observer-observed.

2. This level of Consciousness is knowable by human beings through *experience.*

3. The need to experience this level of Consciousness, beyond a doubt, is an innate drive in the human psyche.

4. Experiential awareness of the Facticity of Opposites can cause a transformation in the human psyche and the emergence of a new door to beyond the mind/body phenomena.

Appendix B

Walking Infinity— A Model for Direction Filter Change

". . . Our thinking creates problems that the same level of thinking won't solve . . ."

Albert Einstein

In order to install the option of choicelessness at the unconscious level, it is imperative that the client have the necessary resources from the spiritual level to allow this choice to be received ecologically. It is also important the client knows s/he *wants* this choice of choicelessness and understands it fully. In this way, the majority of conscious objections will have been handled.

Much trance work will usually have been done, and/or much meditation or familiarity with living in sensory experience. Because this work "gaps" out the mind, it is important that the client know how to handle this type of experience comfortably. In other words, the client needs to know how to just "be" with the sensory experience of right now in a comfortable way, i.e., able to relax with the experience of bare attention.

In this type of change work, we're going to work with the Infinity symbol as a representation of the flow of Opposites. This works well since it visually includes a place where balance is possible between two extreme points, and allows a constant flow of movement back and forth.

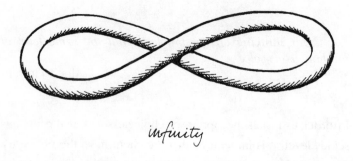

infinity

The first step is to identify the set of opposites being worked with. Then lay out the Infinity symbol and have the client step into the centerpoint and point out which opposite is at which end. Then have the client describe those places with *detailed sub-modalities*. Watch closely for physiology (BMIR's).

If the physiology is very strong, you will have to have full and powerful resources anchored before the client walks the infinity loop fully associated.

Have client step off the loop and establish how they want to relate to these two experiences of living. Positive intention and value of each experience will have to be clarified and established, if you have not already done so. If PS (problem state) physiology is very strong, you may have to create several meta positions. It is important to make each succeeding meta position literally higher than the last. In this situation, we used stools of differing heights.

Have client establish what resources they will need to get that outcome. Have them go on time line and get those resources — both in the past and in the future when new situation is already established.

When resources are anchored and resource state physiology exceeding problem state physiology in intensity, client can walk the infinity loop with resource anchors being held, being sure to begin walking upward into the new experience each time it arises. After a while s/he can switch directions and continue walking. As s/he walks, the practitioner holds the resource anchor and walks with her, for at least two rounds, to make sure the flow continues going on. Simultaneously, the practitioner is using trance language to solidify the shifts and changes happening as the walk continues, familiarizing the client with the feel of this new choice of letting both states be what they are — not pulled toward the positive one, nor avoiding the negative one.

When client wants to stop, have them step off loop at the centerpoint into meta position and get feedback.

Then have them step on time line in the present and walk forward into future with infinity loop underneath them, imagining it going on and on beneath them as they walk unaffected into the future as far as they comfortably can — then turn and look back to the past and walk back as far as they need to go taking the resources with them and healing all the wounds left back there by the original misunderstanding. (Make sure Infinity Loop is continuing there beneath their feet as they walk.) When they reach the beginning point, have them turn toward future and see how the new future looks now and send the new understanding forward into that future solidifying the new perception and seeding the new choice through out all time. Then have the client walk forward, creating new future memories on the time line. Infinity loop is continuing to flow beneath the feet with every step, while the client remains balanced in the centerpoint. Have client then walk back to now, giving this gift of learning and expansion to that one in the present there and then step off the line at the present into meta.

Get feedback from meta position about the one who did all this there on the time line. Then have client go and stand in the middle of the infinity loop in the present and report the submodalities as they appear now. They should be dramatically different in substance and feel.

It is essential in this work to continue strengthening the client's dis-identification with the person who is walking on the Loop (i.e., in time and space) who has to experience the flow of Opposites in the mind and the body. To do this, particular attention must be paid to perceptual positions, and the strengthening of those differing points of view through language.

Transcript from demonstration:

Walking Infinity — Chiara and Ragini

R. Chiara, what would you like to work with?

C. Acceptance and non-acceptance.

R. What's the opposite of acceptance that's not a negation.

C. Non-acceptance — uh, I don't know — what is it?

R. How about rejection?

C. Oh yeah, that's right. *(blushed)*

R. Is that OK to work with then? Acceptance and rejection?

C. Yeah.

R. Can you see the infinity loop there? *(R. has already laid this out on the floor in front of her with a piece of black yarn. She nods yes.)*

R. Will you step onto the centerpoint there and indicate to me which end is acceptance and which end is rejection? *(She steps onto the center point and points to the right for acceptance and to the left for rejection.)*

R. Can you describe to me what you experience there?

C. This end *(she's pointing to acceptance)* is extremely soft and rounded and warm and sticky and smells like honey. It's the color of honey. And it's like mother's milk. It looks and feels like mother's breast. I feel so strongly pulled. *(Physiology very intense here)* I want it. I feel almost woozy. And there's a hum coming from it and a heart beat. But it feels all sappy and drippy.

R. And what is the other end like?

C. Oh, it's so cold and sharp. It has a metal feel, like it has many points, like thorns. It's the color of a gun, and it sounds like the clamor of metal arms, you know, armor.

It so's hard. I feel really terrified by it It's really dark colored. I don't want to get near it. *(Her physiology is again very strong.)*

R. OK, you can step off the centerpoint now and move out here *(pointing to #1 meta position situated on a low stool).* Now Chiara, how do you want her over there to relate to these two experiences?

C. She needs to have a point of view just like standing on the edge of a coin where she can see this from higher up and I can relate to it with some kind of balance. *(She is still being pulled into the physiology of the two states as evidenced by changes in her own physiology and the shift in her language from "she" to "I".)*

R. Chiara, step over here *(pointing to #2 meta position on top of a slightly higher stool)* and get even more distant *(she moves)* from that you now over there that is watching her there on the Infinity Loop. *(Her physiology markedly changes now into a neutral state — or I hallucinated relieved. She gave a big gasp as she looked back at herself watching the loop from #1 meta).*

C. What an insight! I didn't realize she didn't know it was possible to be free of that pattern! *(Her physiology started to change again as she spoke)* I keep seeing these great big hooks coming my way, and I see this big fish mouth like a fish head going to bite on the hooks *(she demonstrates biting into a hook and being pulled along with her own mouth and hand)* and I've been wanting to step off to the side and let these hooks run their course without me getting hooked.

R. Can you make the fish and the hooks smaller now? *(She nods yes simultaneous with a sigh and relaxation of facial tension.)*

C. It's not in my face anymore. But I feel I need to be more spacious. *(She waves her arms around.)*

R. Why don't you move over here and get that different point of view she needs from a higher perspective. *(She moves to the position indicated which is now #3 meta position, located on a slightly higher stool than the other two.)*

C. She needs to be like on the 30th floor of the Columbia building and look down, and she needs to be able to see the textures and the differences in the landscape and relate to them all in the same way. *(As she spoke, she took on yet another physiology — posture straight, head held up, breathing even, voice with an even rhythm and quiet volume)*

R. Have you ever had that kind of experience, Chiara, seeing from that heightened perspective?

C. Yes, numerous times now, but I don't really trust it. *(She still was reproducing some PS physiology each time she looked at the infinity loop.)*

R. Chiara, let's take up the loop for awhile now, is that OK?

C. Oh yes! *(We removed the loop.)*

R. And let's put down your time line. Which way is your past? *(We set up past, present and future.)* OK. Now Chiara, can you think of times in your life when you did trust your experience? *(She wrinkled her nose and squinted her eyes.)* How about trusting your hands when you

197

massage? *(She is a very successful massage practitioner and teacher)* Take a look through your past there and notice what comes up.

C. Yes, I have a few times I really trusted them.

R. OK, then I want you to find the most powerful experience of that on your time line and step into it, really feeling it fully right now. *(She found one or two that we anchored, but even stacking the experiences, the physiology was not stronger than the PS physiology)* Come back over here to this position, Chiara. *(indicating #3 meta)* Can you think of a time when you had that heightened perspective and really were above it all? Does that happen when you're engaged in your spiritual practice?

C. Oh yes, my goodness, when I'm standing in the meditation hall and dancing. I know I can trust my experience then, I can feel my body knowing what to do to let the dancing happen. It's so luscious! *(R. has her go to time line for experiences and anchors them.)*

R. Now Chiara, taking those with you, *(holds both anchors)*, step on your time line and walk to that future point where trust has already happened *(she moves and a new physiology arises)*. Then go even further into the future and find where you trust even a little more. *(She moves forward again.)*

C. I don't really trust this place. It doesn't seem as real as back there. I trusted that one more.

R. OK, step over here *(R. indicates #3 meta position.)*

C. Oh, I want to add to it. I just remembered I found something yesterday.

R. Where did it happen on your time line? *(She points and then steps in.)*

C. Yes, I found this window. I can feel it now, and my being is translucent and transparent with this huge window on nature, and I see trees and I see different colors and different textures and the wind blows and I feel like 3-dimensional inside. A lot of breath and a lot of space and the wind moves through nature like the breath moves through me and it's the whole universe — inside me — *(her voice is slower and slower and punctuated with big breaths and sighs)* I feel so rested inside because I am connected with the inside, I know who I am and where I come from. And I am a universe unto myself and the universes around me are just that — unto themselves. *(R. anchors away!!)* I feel like a tree surrounded by trees and whether they lose their leaves at a different time, or bend with the wind in a different rhythm, that doesn't matter to me here cause I am my own tree, and their dance doesn't effect my dance. We can dance together. *(Resource physiology is now more intense than PS physiology — anchored and OK to go ahead with infinity walk.)*

R. OK Chiara, keeping that with you now, in a moment you're going to move up to the present and as you look forward there, you can see the infinity loop is also there now. *(The yarn is only used once in the beginning to give the client the shape of the infinity loop)* And as you walk forward to that centerpoint, you can know this moves with you now *(holding anchors)*. *(She reaches the centerpoint of the infinity loop which is the present and stops.)* Now Chiara, you can go ahead and walk that loop knowing that as you do, you are taking these resources with you now, that heightened perspective, that trust in your experience, that knowing that you are you, a universe unto yourself (*R. makes sure that Chiara begins moving upward into the side she leans toward first. This is in keeping with kinesiology studies that indicate going upward brings the physiology upwards.*) — and as you walk into acceptance (*she is moving now with R. gently guiding her, R. acting as the force of existence moving Chiara through the Facticity of Opposites as R. holds the anchors* — *hypnotic language continues being given*) you can feel these resources, now yours, melting that stickiness into a smooth passage way through which you are passing now with ease, allowing that pull toward acceptance to continue dissolving more and more with every step as you watch from this place above it all, that heightened perspective that has become yours now, hasn't it . . . and as you move into that experience of rejection now, staying fully in this feeling of spacious independence, free to be you as you are, you can watch that pain and those unpleasant feelings becoming easier and easier to allow as you watch from this place above it all, noticing the textures and the colors and the changing movement as it goes on . . . (*As she continues walking, her physiology determines what is said and how long R. continues holding the anchors and speaking. The Resource physiology keeps growing the more she walks.*)

C. In the beginning, I could really feel more pull toward acceptance and less availability to walk the rejection side, but now, very quickly, I'm starting to get the hang of it. (*Her voice is very breathy and slow and punctuated with sighs and gasps.)* I can feel the new perspective now, I can look down and see what I liked and disliked from different points and yet I can walk around it in stride. It's amazing. It's like getting a dance down. Can I change directions? *(R. indicates that is fine.)* Wow, this really feels like a different point of view even, a different way to approach it and I can still do it. I feel like I'm getting it down. New steps to a new dance.

(She walked around and around for about 4 minutes and then stopped at centerpoint.)

R. How does that feel, Chiara?

C. Wonderful! Amazing!

R. Chiara, I want you to walk now into the future knowing this flow of acceptance and rejection is still going on and moving with you, even as you move onward, and you'll continue being aware of that infinite flow going on beneath your feet with every step you take. And notice how you feel fine as you walk into that future taking this feeling and this knowing with you can trust your experience now, Chiara, haven't you? *(At this point, as she slowly walks, R. begins whispering in her ear the voice of mother's milk & honey, and in the other ear whispering the clamor and the clanging of rejection. She laughs and smiles and says to R.)*

C. Oh, Shut up — Oh, I can turn down the volume of acceptance! Wow! *(She turns towards the acceptance side and with her hand reaches out and turns her hand as if turning a knob.)*

R. How does that feel, Chiara?

C. Sooo good!

R. Great. Now can you turn toward the past, Chiara, and come back to now, keeping these resources *(touches anchors once again)* with you now, Chiara, because they're yours, just like a tree has its own roots and its own branches and leaves *(She smiles, and breaths deeply)* and blossoms in its own time. And I'd like you to just drift back to those places in that past that needed this heightened perspective, this spaciousness, this knowing that you are you and a dance is all it is, and when you find those places, you can stop there, Chiara, and share with that younger or older you *(reference to past lives already established as part of her map)* what you know now and didn't know then can become the now of then, freeing then to become filled with the sights and sounds and smells of this new now, hasn't it? And you might even have to go as far back as some past lives, and if you do, that's OK. *(She reached the end of her time line.)*

C. This is the beginning of time.

R. OK, Chiara, turn around and face that new future there before you *(She very slowly turns continuing to take deep breaths, some tears falling).* And as you feel ready now, you can walk on towards that future, aware of the infinite flow of acceptance and rejection just there beneath you with every step, feeling the healing power of what you've given to yourselves here today. *(She begins to walk slowly, continuing to occasionally breath deeply, arms open wide and her hands are palms up.)* That's right, Chiara, and as you walk forward through time, recognizing that acceptance and rejection continue occurring even now as part of the journey and feeling that freedom from the pull, that freedom from the fear, each step causing your unconscious mind to solidify its learnings here today freeing you to automatically and comfortably shift to that heightened perspective now at even the slightest hint of acceptance beckoning you forward and rejection reaching out to hook you with its pain will cause that shift upwards to reach that higher perspective, like looking out the 30th floor of a tall building, able to notice the different textures and landscapes and relating to them all with the same feeling of freedom. *(Watching for old PS physiology here — testing — only see an intensifying of Resource physiology.)*

And as you walk now, Chiara, aware of that infinity loop beneath your feet with each step, aware of that constant flow between acceptance and rejection, allowing the learning to continue deeply, that feel of just allowing the flow of acceptance and rejection now can continue on its own, as you move in your own rhythm now, going ahead and sending these new learnings and understandings all the way throughout your future there, seeding them throughout all time, knowing they await you there in those future memories taking shape and form even now. *(She walks into the future, stopping here and there at R.'s guidance to form future memories there.)* Now Chiara, you can turn and keeping that strengthened feeling of knowing you can trust this experience as yours, walk to the present and give this present to yourself in the now awaiting your arrival here, knowing she's been waiting a long time to reach you and that time is here now. *(She walks to the present, smiling, with tears.)* And now Chiara, you can step off the time line over here *(pointing to #1 meta)*. How is she doing now? *(R. is pointing to the present point on the time line.)*

C. Absolutely great! She's not sure what's happened, but she certainly feels better.

R. Chiara, will you stand again in the center of the infinity loop and describe to me what she experiences now when she looks at acceptance and at rejection. *(She moves to the centerpoint, her physiology shifting almost immediately to the resource state.)*

C. Wow, it's amazing. They've both sort of leveled out. Acceptance isn't sticky anymore. In fact, it looks childish. *(She giggles and breaths deep.)* This is about growing up, isn't it? I mean the colors are still there. The smoothness is still there. I can still smell the honey, but the pull is different. Wow, there isn't any pull. It's like a dish you really liked as a kid and now, it's just a dish. *(She dances around a bit, smiling.)*

R. And how about rejection?

C. Well, it isn't pointy and prickly anymore. And the sound is definitely quieter. It's not a clamor anymore . And it doesn't feel pointy and prickly. It just feels like something that doesn't effect me. You know, when you look at barbed wire, you don't necessarily get all bent out of shape on the inside.

R. OK, Chiara. Now I want you to step off the line and come over here *(points to a new position not used before)*. Can you put your hands together with the thumbs and the index fingers touching each other? Great. Now can you go ahead and trace the infinity loop in the air there, being sure to go upward into each side, at first very small and now make it bigger and bigger, stretching out as far as you can to each extreme. That's right. And now, can you make it small again and then bigger and then small, and keep doing this for a minute or so? *(She continues tracing the symbol in the air.)* That's great, Chiara. And can you now open your right hand and begin to trace the infinity loop in your palm with the index finger of your left hand, again, being sure to move upward into each side? *(She follows the directions.)* And now can you do the same thing in the palm of your left hand? OK, Chiara, that's great. By the way, do you want to fold up your infinity loop of acceptance and rejection and take it with you? In case you need it again, you'll have all those learnings and experiences right there as soon as you remember the loop.

C. Yes, that's a wonderful idea.

R. Thanks a lot, Chiara.

C. Thank you. (She walks back to her seat smiling widely.)

Two days later:

R. Have you noticed anything in the last two days, Chiara?

C. It's like I can't wait to get the challenge of it! Then last night I had some stuff going on with my boyfriend. I wasn't getting hooked at all. He was saying well maybe we shouldn't get married if I have this situation, and it was like, well OK, if that's what's going on for you. The feelings were there but the hooks weren't. Normally I would have felt rejected and then despair, and then that space where you want to please someone so they'll do what you want. That would have been there in the past. And it wasn't there anymore. Even today with clients, I was completely out of rapport with one of them. Everything I said was wrong, but it was OK. I just relaxed with it and then by the end, rapport was back and everything was fine. I didn't freak out at all. It was a big difference for me.

Two weeks later:

R. How are things going now, Chiara, after two weeks? Anything to report?

C. Yes, just two days ago, I had an amazing test for this. I met a woman I'd known long ago who really never liked me at all and in fact was always quite rude to me. But when I saw her, I said Hi, like you would to someone you knew long ago, and reintroduced myself and boy, she was really cold and distant and obviously still holding a lot against me. And I was surprised to find myself feeling sadness that this was the way it was. No aversion or pull to get away, no old patterns of trying to please her or find out what she wanted. It was amazing. I just finished the conversation and went on, and I knew the sadness was appropriate. Sort of a sign that I was somehow accepting that was the way it was. It was really great, and it surprised me. That was the kind of situation that always got me hooked badly in the past. I feel something very deep has shifted around those issues, and it feels great.

Two months later:

R. How is everything, Chiara, after two months?

C. It's amazing how many times I've noticed myself behaving differently, in my relationship, in my work, and it even seems I'm just more aware these days of opposites in general. In fact, I think that infinity walk shifted a lot of things. I don't know how, but I'm somehow remembering a lot more often to just relax and not take it all too seriously. I did have to pull out my loop once when I was in a real sour situation with my boyfriend, but it was amazing how it helped me to come back to myself almost immediately. Since then, I feel like I've just moved into deeper and deeper levels of understanding about acceptance and rejection, uncovering a lot more things to relax with, of course. There's a new sweetness now, though, even to my painful times. I think something is still going on cause I'm almost hungry for more meditation in my life. And that's incredible in itself!

Steps For Direction Filter Change:

1. Establish set of opposites to be worked with and presence of infinity loop. Have client step onto loop and describe sub-modalities of each extreme in detail.

2. Establish new way in which client wishes to relate to this never ending flow of seeming opposites. (Desired Outcome)

3. Establish resources needed to reach this new way of relating to these opposites. Evoke and anchor via time line.

4. With resources, have client walk the infinity loop, experiencing this new response. Walk should continue until all PS physiology has disappeared. If objections arise at any time, recycle back to step 3, and handle objection in whatever way is appropriate. Then, continue on.

5. Guide client to walk forward on the time line with infinity loop flowing beneath their feet as they walk, strengthening this new response as they move into the future. Then, have them walk into the past, healing old wounds arising from that misunderstanding about opposites with the power of this new response. When they reach the originating point, have them turn again to the future and send all the new learnings forward through time, preparing everyone there to go on now. Have them walk into future and create future memories as they go. Then, turn and go back to now, giving present self the gift of this new response. All of this work is to be supported by on-going hypnotic language patterns and suggestion.

6. Have client step off the time line at present and go to meta. Get feedback about how that one on the time line is doing with this new change.

7. Have client step back on the time line at the present and describe the sub-modalities as they appear now.

8. Have client hold hands together with index fingers and thumbs touching, forming a triangle space between the hands. Then have them trace the infinity loop in the air in front of them, making it small at first and then as big as they can, stretching as far to each extreme as possible, then small again, then big, continuing on for about a minute. Then have them trace the infinity loop in the palm of their right hand with their finger and then in the palm of the left hand with their other finger. This is from kinesiology and helps to establish the new pattern.

Steps For Direction Filter Change Including Belief Change:

This model requires previous trance work to elicit and solidify resources from the spiritual level and the answering of unconscious objections to relaxing with duality. When this is done, this model works very easily, and well with groups.

Creating meta positions that are physically higher than the one before simulates the logical levels, i.e., behavior and environment are anchored to the infinity symbol, capabilities are anchored to the #1 meta position, beliefs & values anchored to the #2 meta position, and #3 meta position anchors identity to information and experience from the spiritual level — a place very distant from identification with the old mind and its perception of seeming opposites.

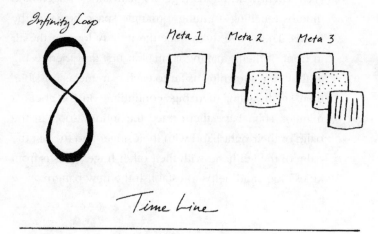

---

1. Establish set of opposites to be worked with and the presence of infinity loop with three meta positions behind it, each one progressively higher, with the first being higher than the infinity loop. Have client step onto loop, locate which end of the loop is which opposite and then describe the sub-modalities of each extreme in detail.

2. Establish new way in which client wishes to relate to this never ending flow of life experience by having them step backwards into the #1 meta position which should be higher than the loop spread on the floor, leaving the self completely identified with the mind and its perceptions of opposites there on the loop.

3. From this meta position, establish the resources needed for the one waiting on the loop to reach this new way of relating to these opposites.

4. Establish the client's time line to the side of the original lay-out. Evoke and anchor the desired resources by having client step inside the feel of each resource, following the feeling back through time, stopping at each point where it is strongest. Each time they stop, anchor the experience, stacking resources as they go.

5. Have client return to #1 meta position with resources intact. Then have them step back again into #2 meta position which is higher still. From here, a greater distance and a broader view is available and they can see what, if any, beliefs might stop or hinder the one on the loop, identified with the mind, from behaving in the new way, even with the desired resources, or the one standing in #1 meta position, a little distanced from the mind/body and watching the one on the loop, fully identified.

6. When conflicting beliefs come into awareness for either of the two positions being watched, prepare the client to ready themselves to step into the highest level of their spiritual understandings yet, both conscious and unconscious, and discover what insight or understanding is going to dissolve that belief and destroy its hold.

7. When ready, have the client step to the highest #3 meta position, and reveal what arises and how they can see from this perspective new points of view that dissolve the old beliefs of the one standing just in front now in the position #2, as well as beliefs of the one in the #1 meta position, and the one on the infinity loop itself. As these insights and understandings arise and are verbalized, anchor them. Be sure client always speaks about

the other positions as "he" or "she", and your hypnotic language reinforces these differing positions of identification which are also now spatially anchored.

8. Holding the spiritual insight anchor, guide the client down into the #2 meta position and with hypnotic language support the dissolution of the old belief and the entrance of the spiritual insight or understanding into this position, bringing these insights closer and closer now to the one on the loop fully identified with the mind/body. When physiology indicates this is finished, prepare client to bring these spiritual insights even closer now to the one destined to live in the mind/body and walk the infinity loop.

9. Still holding spiritual insight anchor, guide the client into the #1 meta position, and check if the resources first chosen are still appropriate in light of these new insights and understandings and the dissolving of the old beliefs. If there is any change or addition, handle it now.

10. When the client is ready to bring these resources and spiritual insights and understandings right into the one identified with the mind/body, continue holding spiritual insight anchor and fire resource anchor as you guide them to step into the one waiting there at the centerpoint of the loop and begin to guide them to walk the loop, going upward into the experiences, anchors held, guiding them physically for at least two rounds. Then let go of the anchors, and allow the client to walk the loop at varying speeds and rhythms, differing directions as well as backwards and forwards. Walk should continue until all PS physiology disappears.

11. Standing at the centerpoint, have client imagine a moment of forgetfulness arising, beginning to feel a pull into the old identification with the mind and the fight with opposites. As they begin, pull them immediately off the loop and up the series of meta positions to the highest level (#3), reclaiming the knowings that are now theirs. Firing the anchors once again, bring them quickly back down to the one on the loop and have them notice how it feels to so quickly remember what they know. (Do this according to physiology, of course.) Continue this for several trips up and back down, continuing to install this new pattern of response to the old PS.

12. Guiding client to the time line, continue as in step 5 in the first model above all the way through.

Facticity, in its varying stages of development, has been experienced by over 500 people as of the time of this writing. The majority of these people, considering themselves meditators and seekers, are reporting impactful changes in their behavior, immediately and over time.

Appendix C

Five Minute Consciousness Expander

Please be aware Facticity addresses a high level human need and would be inappropriate at this stage of its development for individuals who are not relatively stable both mentally and emotionally, i.e., very functional.

We are using Facticity to install the following process at the unconscious level of the mind as soon as the perception of a problem, stress, or undesired emotional state arises.

1. Say to yourself, "Stop a moment. Stress means I'm not relaxing with something as it is. I want to relax and flow with life whatever it is bringing me."

2. Step inside the problem (feel it). Then step outside and ask, "What is the value s/he is seeking to fulfill there by behaving in that manner?"

3. Ask, "What old and currently unconscious belief is driving her to support this value?"

4. Ask, "What set of opposites is in play in this dynamic?"

5. Ask, "Which opposite is being supported or valued by her actions and which opposite is being denied or devalued?"

6. Ask, "What is the positive value of the denied opposite? How is its presence useful and necessary to her in receiving the presence of the valued opposite?"

7. What is the new value you would like to support now.

8. Find something in nature, inside or out, providing undeniable evidence of both opposites actually working together or being complementary.

9. Make an image of both outcomes: how s/he will feel choosing one opposite over the other, and how s/he will feel accepting both and allowing each to have its value and function in supporting the presence of the other.

10. Shift your attention back and forth from one to the other, noticing how choosing leads her to the same stress-filled reactions of the past and a feel of disharmony. Notice how choicelessness leads her to a future of relaxation now and a feel of being free to harmonize with and accept things as they are moment to moment.

11. Consciously shift your attention now to the choice of choicelessness and step inside that outcome, noticing how the perception of a "problem" has disappeared.

    If there are objections, cycle back to #8 to uncover more undeniable evidence of the Facticity of Opposites relevant to this situation.

CONTENT EXAMPLE OF FIVE MINUTE CONSCIOUSNESS EXPANDER

The problem is, "I'm feeling alone and I want to be together with my friend."

1. Stop for a moment. Stress means I'm not relaxing with something as it is. I want to relax and flow with life, whatever it is bringing me.

2. As I look at her over there, the value she is seeking to fulfill here is acceptance and when she is alone, she doesn't feel she is OK.

3. I can see the old and unconscious belief driving her to support this value says, "Togetherness is the way to be happy and to know that you are OK."

4. I'm aware the opposites in play in this dynamic are aloneness and togetherness.

5. Togetherness is being supported and valued through her actions and aloneness is being denied and devalued.

6. Aloneness is valuable to me now because it is where I fill up from the inside, know I'm OK, and then have something to share. Aloneness allows togetherness to be fresh and new each time we come together.

7. The new value I'd like to support now is awareness and relaxation with what life is giving me.

8. It is undeniably true that each bird flying in the sky has to fly under the power of his own two wings and that no matter how many birds choose to fly together, when it's time to migrate together or play together, each bird still flies alone, in his own space and with his own wings.

9. I can see her continuing to choose togetherness over aloneness and continuing to feel bad and rejected and not OK, as she has felt seemingly forever. I can see her relaxing with both experiences, aware of a knowing that coming together and going apart is the natural rhythm of relationship, and with this awareness, I can see her relaxing and using her alone time to continue exploring her creative expressions.

10. As I shift back and forth between the two, I can see and feel that the choice of choosing makes her feel bad and the choice of choicelessness leaves space for many other things to arise, especially giving her a new sense of self-respect and dignity.

11. I will consciously step in the choice of choicelessness now and continue learning this feel of relaxing and accepting what life is bringing my way.

Notes:

Glossary

Apposition of Opposites: a linguistic form of placing opposites, or opponent systems, together in order to balance those opposites in a manner useful to the hypnotic process. For example, "As your arm lifts, your leg will feel heavy." This form *utilizes* the natural tendency of the system to create the opposite of what is being requested, i.e., heaviness when lightness is being suggested, by offering the heaviness a place to be useful and reinforcing of the desired response.

Attention Filter: a specific unconscious meta-program or filter that tells us where to direct our attention, to self or others, inside or outside.

Content-Free Meditation: a technique of experiencing mental, physical and emotional processes from a meta position (watching, witnessing). In Facticity, this is used to evoke and develop the mental capacity of non-judgemental awareness.

Deletion, Distortion, Generalization: three basic unconscious processes to which all sensory input is subject. In its useful form, deletion keeps out of awareness sensory stimuli unnecessary for survival. Distortion is necessary for creative visualization and imagination. Generalization is also useful as when we touch a hot stove and generalize the experience to all hot stoves, saving us from the same painful experiences in the future. In its non-useful form, deletion can cause us to overlook experiences that do not support our beliefs or ideas.

Distortion can cause us to translate experience so it fits our limiting beliefs. Generalization can cause us to over-generalize, creating limiting mindsets.

Direction Filter: a specific unconscious meta-program or filter that directs our response to experience by causing us to either move toward the experience, usually perceived as positive, or to move away from the experience, usually perceived as negative.

Embedded Suggestion: a form of indirect suggestion that offers a direct suggestion embedded within another context. For example, "A bud beginning to open could **feel good** about that experience."

Ericksonian Hypnosis: the most modern developments in hypnosis are currently credited to Milton H. Erickson, M.D. whose contributions form the body of what is commonly called the permissive approach to hypnosis, rather than the traditional approach coined authoritarian. Permissive comes from a style that directly guides the subject to the desired outcome in a variety of indirect ways, simultaneously providing the subject with a psychological feeling of freedom to travel to the desired outcome in their own way. Ericksonian Hypnosis is also noted for *actively* evoking and engaging the abilities of the subject's unconscious mind in creating the desired change. Dr. Ernest Rossi, Richard Bandler, John Grinder and others, have studied Dr. Erickson and his work pinpointing and identifying specific skills and techniques basic to this style.

Indirect Associative Focusing: is a basic form of indirect suggestion, usually given via metaphor. The relevant topic is brought up without any specific reference to the client, thereby triggering a spontaneous unconscious search for associations with that topic that are personal to the listener (TDS). This manner of presentation usually bypasses conscious limitations/objections/defenses. If the relevant topic is, in fact, not a relevant aspect of the subject's problem, nothing is lost. If it is, the subject will begin to talk about it, perhaps without any conscious awareness of doing so as a response to the suggestions. To a large degree, this approach can avoid imposing the presenter's personal views upon the client. For example, if you want to indirectly focus someone's attention on asking you for a date, you can speak about many different experiences of being out, by yourself and with companions, having a good time, baking a fruit cake with a good friend, checking appointments in your calendar book. "Dates" are a thread connecting each of the seemingly disconnected anecdotes. If the other is interested in asking you out, the unconscious mind will probably receive the message about dates and then proceed to do so.

Meaning Making Process: another reference to TDS, or the unconscious search for meaning.

Meta-Programs: a deep level of unconscious mental programming or filtering that determines how we basically relate to, or attend to our experiences. These include programming or filters that create our orientation toward goals and problems, relationships, time, and organization of information.

NLP: Neuro-Linguistic Programming is a body of knowledge and a set of skills based on behavioral modeling co-created by Richard Bandler and John Grinder. It is commonly defined as the study of the structure of human subjectivity. It relates to knowledge of how patterns (programming) arise from an interaction between our brain/body (neuro/physiology) and words (linguistic) and thus affect our behavior.

Nominalization: an unconscious linguistic process of changing a verb into a noun. For example, we unconsciously change the process of deciding into a decision. We unconsciously change the process of relating into a relationship A nominalization is a violation of what is called the Meta Model, a linguistic model developed by Grinder and Bandler that identifies categories of language patterns and how they can become a problem.

Phonological Ambiguity: utilizes the fact that certain words with distinct meaning are represented with the same sequence of sound. For example, hand can be both the physical part of the body or the verb meaning to give something to someone. Use of this form of ambiguity triggers the TDS process (search for meaning). For example, "What's it like to give a hand to someone just met?" Does this mean help them with something or stretch out the hand for a handshake? Ambiguity is very helpful in pacing and leading clients in trance work.

Presupposition: is a sentence assumed to be true in order for another sentence to make sense. Presuppositions are usually at the unconscious level or outside conscious awareness. For example, in the sentence, "Mind is the enemy of meditation", the unconscious mind must assume as true that mind exists,

that meditation exists, that enemies exist, that there are enemies of meditation, and that there is a relationship between
mind and meditation. Upon recognition of the Facticity of
Opposites, the unconscious mind will also recognize that if
mind is the enemy of meditation, then mind can also be a
friend to meditation, and if meditation has enemies, then
meditation can also have friends.

Punctuation Ambiguity: utilizes the final word in a sequence
of words as the first word of a different sequence of words with
another meaning. "And you can find that position of comfort
can arise now." Punctuation ambiguity can also utilize phonological ambiguity in a specific structure. For example, "That's a
nice watch my hand closely."

Sorting Programs: is another name for meta-programs. It is
also commonly used to refer to that meta program that sorts
experience by matching (sorting for similarities) or mis-matching (sorting for differences). For example, when you walk into
a new restaurant, do you notice what is similar to your favorite
restaurant, or do you notice what is different?

Sub-Modalities: are sub-categories of each sensory mode and
identify the special sensory qualities of each sense. For example, some of the kinesthetic sub-modalities include temperature, pressure, texture and weight. Some of the visual sub-
modalities include brightness, distance, location and movement. Some of the auditory sub-modalities include volume,
tempo, pitch and distance. Sub-modalities are referred to as the
universal building blocks of subjective experience. In other

words, these are the basic building blocks that make up our sensory experience. Every sensory experience we have is composed of these elements in some combination or another.

Suggestions Covering All Possibilities of a Class of Response: Suggestions coverings all possibilities of a class of response actually restrict the subject to a fairly narrow range of response, yet creates the feeling of psychological choice. For example, "And in a few moments, you can feel yourself relaxing. And how will that relaxation appear? In eyes that get heavy and tired and want to close? Or will it be a feeling of heaviness in the arms and legs? Or perhaps that sensation of lightness as the release of tension goes on, causing a feeling of floating or drifting there, comfortable and quiet?" The direct suggestion here is "feel yourself relaxing", but the subject will feel great freedom to create that relaxation in their own way.

TDS: Transderivational Search is the unconscious process of searching back through stored mental information to find a reference experience from which a current behavior or response derives its meaning. In hypnosis, it is commonly called the unconscious search for meaning. In order to understand what another is saying, and whether it is relevant to the subject or not, the unconscious mind must engage in this automatic and unconscious search for meaning. Certain language patterns will automatically trigger this search engaging the unconscious mind to be actively involved (a mark of the Ericksonian approach). For example, when the unconscious mind hears, "Some people grasp Facticity more easily than others", it will automatically search to discover whether that statement is relevant to the listener. Which people? Is she talking about me? Am I one who's grasping it more easily than others?

Universal Building Blocks of Experience: is another way to refer to sub-modalities. In order for a sensory experience to exist in the mind, it will be built (re-presented) by the sensory qualities known as sub-modalities.

Bibliography

General References:

Capra, F. *The Tao Of Physics*, Berkeley, CA: Shambhala Press, 1975.

Daumal, Rene *Mount Analogue*, CA: Shambhala Press, 1981.

Goldstein, Joseph *The Experience of Insight*, Santa Cruz, CA: Unity Press, 1976.

Kornfield, Jack *Living Buddhist Masters*, Santa Cruz, CA: Unity Press, 1977.

Krishnamurti, J. *Freedom From The Known*, San Francisco, CA: Harper, 1969.

Krishnamurti, J. *Meditations*, India: Krishnamurti Foundation India, 1979.

Levine, S. *A Gradual Awakening*, New York: Anchor Books, 1979.

Merrell-Wolff, F. *The Philosophy of Consciousness Without An Object*, New York: The Julian Press, 1973.

Merton, Thomas *The Way of Chuang Tzu*, New York: New Directions, 1965.

Michaels, R.E. *Lions In Wait*, Seattle, WA: Facticity Trainings, Inc., 1992.

Michaels, R.E. *Storytelling The Truth*, (pending final publication 1992).

Osho, *Hidden Harmony (on Heraclitus)*, India: Rajneesh Foundation, 1976.

Osho, *When The Shoe Fits (on Chuang Tzu)*, India: Rajneesh Foundation, 1977.

Osho, *Neither This Nor That (on 3rd Zen Patriarch)*, India: Rajneesh Foundation, 1975.

Reps, Paul *Zen Flesh, Zen Bones*, New York: Anchor Books, Doubleday, A233.

Sujata, A. *Beginning to See*, Santa Cruz, CA: Unity Press, 1975.

Suzuki, S. *Zen Mind, Beginner's Mind*, New York: Weatherhill, Inc., 1970.

NLP and Ericksonian References:

Andreas, C. & S. *The Heart Of The Mind*, Utah: Real People Press, 1989.

Bandler, R. *Use Your Brain For A Change*, Utah: Real People Press, 1985.

Bandler, R. & Grinder, J. *The Structure of Magic, I & II*, Palo Alto, CA: Science and Behavior Books, 1975.

Bandler, R. & Grinder, J. *Patterns I*, Cupertino, CA: Meta Publications, 1975.

Bandler, R. & Grinder, J. *Tranceformations*, Utah: Real People Press, 1981.

Dilts R. *Changing Beliefs with NLP,* Cupertino, CA: Meta Publications, 1990.

Erickson, Milton H. *Healing In Hypnosis,* New York: Irvington Publishers, 1983.

Erickson, Milton H. & Edited by Rossi, Ernest L. *The Collected Papers of Milton H. Erickson on Hypnosis, Vol. 1-1V,* New York: Irvington Publishers, 1980.

James, T. *Time Line Therapy and The Basis of Personality,* Cupertino, California: Meta Publications, 1988.

Lewis, B. & Pucelik, F. *Magic Demystified,* Lake Oswego, OR: Metamorphous Press, 1982.

O'Hanlon, W. H. *Tap Roots,* New York: Norton & Co., 1987.

Ornstein, R. Ph.D. & Sobel, D. M.D. *The Healing Brain,* New York: Simon & Schuster, 1987.

Rossi, Ernest L. & Erickson, Milton H. *Hypnotic Realities,* New York: Irvington Publishers, 1976.

About the Author

Ragini Elizabeth Michaels has been working with people as a Clinical Hypnotherapist and a Trainer of NLP and Ericksonian Hypnosis for over eighteen years. She travels worldwide presenting Facticity to a wide variety of audiences. As the author of six critically acclaimed audio tapes and the creator of the Facticity Process (a group experience), Ragini relishes in continuing the exploration of new and creative applications of NLP and Hypnosis to the advancement of human consciousness. Ragini lives in the Pacific Northwest and enjoys spending her leisure time walking, playing music and drawing.

Facticity® Trainings, Inc.

Facticity Trainings is dedicated to the support and advancement of human consciousness in the fields of communication and behavioral change. Our commitment to evoking conscious awareness, as well as excellence and elegance in the training and performance of Practitioners of NLP and Hypnosis, creates training programs high in quality, self-awareness and heart. Facticity Trainings recognizes that a *better* mind may not be of much value unless non-judgemental awareness and new levels of consciousness are available to guide that mind in the service of the human heart and spirit.

Facticity Trainings offers Certification programs at the Practitioner and Master Practitioner levels of NLP. These programs provide concurrent training in Ericksonian Hypnosis. Programs are also available relating to both an integration of NLP and Massage as well as various business communication trainings.

Facticity Trainings is the publisher of the two critically acclaimed audio tape series *Remembrance* and *Facticity* as well as Ms. Michaels new books to be released in 1992 - *Lions in Wait* and *Storytelling The Truth*.

Facticity Trainings Audio

Acoustic Associative Hypnosis

Each tape offers a side with hypnotic trance accompanied by music as well as a side with just the music alone. Both the *Facticity Series* and *Remembrance Series* tapes take the idea of subliminal hypnosis one step further.

Subliminal tapes provide a voice outside the individual telling the person what to do. Acoustic Associative Hypnosis (AAH) evokes your unconscious ability to create by itself the words you need to hear, the images you need to see, and the feelings you want to feel.

After listening to the trance side just a few times, your unconscious will associate the words, and the inner experience they create, with the music. Listening to just the music side will cause your unconscious mind to remember the words and continue utilizing them in the most appropriate way for you.

The dance between Ragini's soothing and melodious voice and Ambodha's inspired and transforming music carries you spaciously and graciously toward whatever depths or heights you're ready to explore.

Facticity tapes utilize Digital Stereo Processing in addition to extended frequency response. Original music is composed, performed, and recorded by Divyam Ambodha. All music has been crafted to work in concert with each tape's theme.

Facticity Series

Beginnings & Endings - Relaxing with Change - works to re-educate your unconscious mind to the presence of change and its hidden pattern of flow from one extreme towards its seeming opposite and back again. A relaxing and soothing reminder that change is natural and you can learn to relax with this flow.

Balancing In Motion - works to strengthen your unconscious mind's awareness that balance is a process, rather than a position to achieve, freeing you to more easily experience that balancing in motion.

Remembrance Series

Answers Rest Within - provides a beautiful and relaxing way to re-educate your unconscious mind to look within for the answers you seek.

Awareness Arising - supports the ability of your unconscious mind to heighten your awareness and allow you to be in the moment - here and now.

Beyond The Past - guides your unconscious mind in how to let go of what is no longer needed, keeping the learnings and freeing you to move beyond those conditionings of long ago.

Healing Heart - works to heal wounds of the heart and evoke the heart's capacity to forgive, to accept and to allow the love to flow.

Reviews

"I would recommend these tapes to any of my students ... Ragini Michaels has excellent control of the subtleties of this art."
Nancy L. Beplat, Rapporter, Nov-Dec 1990

"Ragini's tapes certainly are fine examples of Ericksonian trance induction techniques and allowed me to quickly and easily drift into a relaxed, calm state."
Will MacDonald, NLP Trainer, NLP Northwest
"An Insider's Guide To Sub-Modalities"

"The Facticity tapes have the best music in terms of composition and follow the [Ericksonian] style with the most creative use of language."
Sandy LaForge, Anchor Point, June 1990

Trance-Scripts

Each audio tape in the *Facticity Series* and *Remembrance Series* has been transcribed for those interested in learning the underlying Ericksonian linguistic patterns. These patterns are often referred to as the "Milton Model Language Patterns" and are clearly notated on each transcription. There is one Trance-Script for each of the six tapes.

Upcoming Facticity Series Books

Lions In Wait, a book of metaphor, will be available in Spring of 1992. *Storytelling The Truth* will follow in winter of 1992. If you would like advance notice of publication, please check the box on the order form on the following page.

Order Form

	Tape Qty.	Trance-Script Qty.	
	_____	_____	Beginnings & Endings
	_____	_____	Balancing In Motion
	_____	_____	Answers Rest Within
	_____	_____	Awareness Arising
	_____	_____	Beyond The Past
	_____	_____	Healing Heart
	_____	_____	Total(s)

_____ Tape Price (see below)
_____ Trance-Script Price (see below)
_____ Copies of *Facticity - A Door To Mental Health And Beyond* @ $16.95 Each
_____ Shipping & Handling (see below)
_____ Wash. Residents add 8.2% Sales Tax
_____ Total Funds Enclosed

Tape Prices
1 Tape $14.95	3 Tapes $39.95
2 Tapes $26.95	4 Tapes $49.95
5 Or More Tapes $11.95 Each	

Trance-Script Prices
1-3 Trance-Scripts $5.95 Each   4 Or More $4.95 Each

Shipping & Handling - 1st Class/Air
Tapes/Domestic - $1.50 1st Tape, $.50 Each Additional Tape
Tapes/International - $3.00 1st Tape, $1.00 Each Additional Tape
Books/Domestic - $3.50
Books/International - $7.00
Trance-Scripts - Same As Tapes (Domestic & International)

International Orders
Must be American Express International Money Order
or check drawn on banks with a branch in the U.S.A.
Monies must be in US funds only.

❏ Please send information on *NLP and Hypnosis Trainings*
❏ Please send information on *The Facticity Experience*
❏ Please send pre-publication information on *Lions In Wait*

Mail Your Payment to: Facticity Trainings, Inc., Post Office Box 22814, Seattle, WA 98122, U.S.A.   Phone: 206-462-4369

Name (Company Optional)

Address   Apt. #

City   State   Zip

Day Phone   Evening Phone